GOD'S CHILD ANDREW

GOD'S CHILD ANDREW

by
SANDRA JOHNSON

Foreword by
THOMAS HOPKO

With appendix by
METROPOLITAN ANTHONY OF SOUROZH

ST VLADIMIR'S SEMINARY PRESS
CRESTWOOD, NEW YORK 10707
1998

Library of Congress Cataloging-in-Publication Data

Johnson, Sandra, 1954-
    God's child Andrew / by Sandra Johnson: foreword by Thomas Hopko; with an
appendix by Metropolitan Anthony of Sourozh.
        p.   cm.
    Includes bibliographical references.
        1. Johnson, Andrew Stanar. 2. Johnson, Sandra, 1954- . 3. Johnson, Duane Martin.
4. Johnson family—Biography. 5. Orthodox (Orthodox Eastern Church)—United
States—Biography. 6. Children—Death—Religious aspects—Christianity.
7. Death—Religious aspects—Orthodox Eastern Church. 8. Spiritual life—Orthodox
Eastern Church. 9. Orthodox Eastern Church—Doctrines. I. Title.
ISBN 0-88141-181-7
BX738.779.A1J64   1998
261.9'092'273—dc21
[B]   98-15993
                                                                              CIP

Copyright © 1998

St. Vladimir's Seminary Press
575 SCARSDALE RD., CRESTWOOD, NY 10707
1-800-204-2665

The Suffering and Death of Children
© 1984 Metropolitan Anthony of Sourozh

All Rights Reserved

ISBN 0-88141-181-7

PRINTED IN THE UNITED STATES OF AMERICA

Contents

Andrew Johnson

† 1993

...the substance of things hoped for,
the evidence of things not seen...

Hebrews 11:1

Foreword

Compelled by a calling confirmed by her family, friends and spiritual fathers, Sandy Johnson describes the life and death of her son Andrew, and the events that followed. She recounts Andy's childhood, his sudden death in an automobile accident on the way to church, and his presence within his grief-stricken family until the time of her husband's ordination to the priesthood. Fr. Duane Johnson, Andy's father, writes the epilogue to his wife's courageous book.

The only writing more difficult and dangerous than describing the life and death of a blessed child, with its glory and grief, is writing when the child is one's own. The pain and risk of such writing are obvious. God's grace alone allows, and even demands, that they be accepted, suffered and shared.

Sandy and Fr. Duane have accomplished this writing in the most gracious way. They tell Andrew's story, and their own, with awesome simplicity and disarming directness. The result is Christian *martyria* and *homologia* in their purest form: a *witness* and *confession* which must be made, whatever the cost. "For the love of Christ constrains us." (2 Corinthians 5:14)

Andrew's parents are not trying to persuade anyone of anything. They have no desire to instruct, inspire, edify or convince. Like Christ's beloved disciple John, they have rather only an irresistable urging to recount what their eyes have seen, their ears heard, their hands handled, their hearts endured, and their minds and bodies suffered "concerning the word of life." They do this so that we may have communion with them, and that our joy, with theirs, may be full. (Cf. 1 John 1:1-4)

Every human being who lives for even a moment in his or her mother's womb is a unique word spoken by God. Every human face is God's icon. Every human person is God's child. Every human story is ultimately God's own story which finds its deepest meaning, purpose and perfection in God's Child Jesus, the Crucified Christ.

When hearing the story of God's child Andrew, a faithful Christian cannot help but recall the biblical words of *Wisdom*:

> The righteous, though he die early, will be at rest. For old age is not honored for length of time, nor measured by number of years...

> There was one who pleased God and was loved by him, and while living among sinners he was taken up. He was caught up lest evil change his understanding or guile deceive his soul...

> Being perfected in a short time, he fulfilled long years for his soul was well pleasing to the Lord, therefore he took him quickly from the midst of wickedness. (Wisdom 4:7-14)

When meeting Andrew, with his parents, family and friends, we find ourselves also under a certain constraint. We must decide with them what we will do about what we have seen and heard. In reading this little book, which so eloquently demonstrates the coincidence of humility and boldness which are always found where God is, we are compelled to respond to what, or, more accurately, to *whom* we have been given to know. For the words of *Wisdom* continue:

> Yet the peoples saw and did not understand, nor take such a thing to heart, that God's grace and mercy are with his chosen, and he watches over his holy ones.

> For they will see...and will not understand what the Lord purposed for him...

> They will see, and have contempt for him, but the Lord will laugh them to scorn. (Wisdom 4:15-18)

May we honor Andrew's memory and his loved ones' sorrow by seeing, understanding and taking to heart what the Lord purposed for him in his short life. And may we also be blessed to see, understand and take to heart what the Lord purposes for us through the story of Andrew which his mother has now so lovingly entrusted to us.

Fr. Thomas Hopko, Dean
St. Vladimir's Seminary

Introduction

When our son Andrew died, our pastor, Father Ray Velencia wrote these words:

> It is with a very heavy heart that I sit down to write this message. I am grieving the loss of you, Andy. I grieve not for you because I know with every fiber of my being that you are in the glorious presence of our Lord, a place each of us longs to be. I grieve for the loss your death has left us. I grieve for your parents, your sister, your grandparents and family who miss you so terribly. I grieve also for our parish family at St. Matthew who have come to know and love you so deeply, for we will certainly miss you. I do now and always will.

> Andy came to us at St. Matthew in Columbia almost three years ago. I remember Andy as a child who had a lot of energy and a distinct persona. He was one of those people who once you meet, you never forget. He had something very special and unique about him. That sense was unmistakable.

> I came to find out that part of this was in fact due to a very special relationship he had with our Lord, which went much deeper or further than any of us probably realized. His parents knew the depth of Andy's relationship; they lived with our beloved Andy every day. Yet, even they never ceased to be amazed by him.

> As you probably are aware, in many Orthodox churches it is not uncommon for priests to require boys to be a certain age before they can serve as altar boys, usually around seven or eight years of age. At St. Matthew, we have many, many children. However, nearly all the boys are seven years old or younger. In September, we lost Derrick, one of our two teenage altar boys, to relocation after his father was transferred to a job in Texas. When this happened, Sandy came to me at coffee hour after church and informed me that Andy, who was then five years old, really wanted to be an altar boy. Could we give it a try? I said sure. Why not? I must admit to some skepticism about

1

how it would go. The services are long, and being a mission parish, there is no iconostas to hide behind. Everything is out in the open, but, I thought to myself, why not? I would never want to discourage anyone in their zeal, regardless of age, to serve the Lord at His table. So, I told Sandy, sure—let's give it a go. So we did.

Let me tell you that Andy served our Lord's table with more of a sense of understanding, purpose, and reverence, than most, regardless of what age, I have ever seen. I was an altar boy myself at St. Nick's in Steelton, Pennsylvania and remember the high jinks and general demeanor of us all. But from the moment Andy donned his robe and began serving, I knew in my spirit, in the very depths of my being, this was no ordinary five-year-old. This was no ordinary child indeed.

Andy had an aura about him as he served. It was unmistakable. It was truly beautiful and awe-inspiring. From that moment on, I had no doubts. He was something. I knew it, and the people knew it. He loved our Lord in his heart and with all his heart. He had a purity and an experience of Christ which each of us would love to have. He lived for Sundays. He lived to serve our Lord. Such is the legacy and lesson he has left us and taught us.

Andy's pure and radiant joy in serving our Lord is something I pray that each and every one of us would have. That we, too, would live for Sundays. That we would live to serve our Lord. The message of his life rings true and loudly. He has called us, by the example of his faith, to the life of blessedness in Christ.

May we, in our grief over the loss of our beloved Andy, find comfort, faith, and hope in the life he lived in, and for, Christ. May we honor his memory by living the rest of our lives with the same joy, zeal, and sense of purpose that our dear Andy did. In living this way, we shall see him again and be with him for eternity in our Lord's everlasting kingdom. May his memory be eternal. Pray for us dear brother!

With all my love in Christ,
†Fr. Ray Velencia, Priest
The Orthodox Church of St. Matthew

1

The Journey Begins

When I stepped through the classroom door in the autumn of 1982, I had no idea of the magnitude of the change about to take place in my life. I entered Ohio State University as a graduate student in Arabic and Islamic history having finished a five-year career as a journalist, including a stint in Cairo as a foreign correspondent. During my assignment to the Associated Press bureau in Cairo, President Anwar Sadat mounted his historic peace mission to Jerusalem, an initiative that eventually cost him his life. I covered Egypt's reaction to Sadat's trip, including some minor rioting in Cairo's Palestinian community and later wrote about the aftermath of his assassination. A translator had to accompany me on many of my interviews. This disturbed me. How could I be certain that I was reporting the true story if I had to rely upon a translator for information?

After returning to the United States, I reported political and international events, including some pieces on the Iranian hostage crisis. A second factor in my decision to seek my graduate degree occurred during the Iranian hostage crisis. My editors sent me to Jessup, Iowa, for the homecoming celebration for Katherine Koob, one of the diplomats at the American Embassy in Tehran who had been held by her Iranian captors for four hundred and forty-four days. I arrived at the airport with scores of other journalists. Katherine Koob descended from the plane. She stood at a microphone to say a few words to the press and her well-wishers. She then joined her brother who intended to take her home, at last, to her family. My orders were to return with an "exclusive" interview, so I had positioned my car alongside the road just outside the entrance to the airport. As Katherine Koob and her brother moved toward his van, I sprinted to my car and began to follow them. As we drove along the rural roads, it did not take them long to realize that they had an uninvited guest. Her brother pulled his van to the side of the road, and

I also pulled aside. He approached me angrily, asking if the four hundred and forty-four days in captivity had not been enough. I explained that my job depended on a personal interview, and I would follow them until I had it. He went back to the van, and Katherine Koob emerged.

She opened the passenger door of my car and sat down. I apologized and then asked how her experience in captivity had changed her and how she felt about her captors. Katherine Koob said that she spent much of her time in captivity praying, and the experience had moved her closer to God than she had ever been. She did not hate her Muslim captors. She empathized with them, pointing out that we are all bound in faith to a merciful God.

Katherine Koob touched something deep inside me that day. When I entered the newsroom, everyone cheered my cunning in getting the interview. They cheered until I wrote about the quiet spiritual awakening that Katherine Koob had said would shape the rest of her life. Faith in God and prayer did not make headlines, according to my editors. They chastised me severely for not digging deeper. I had already been thinking about taking a temporary leave of absence to pursue my graduate degree and return to the Middle East. So I began exploring scholarship possibilities and not long afterward found myself on the Ohio State University campus.

I walked into my colloquial Arabic language class that first afternoon in a suit with my best businesslike stride. I intended my dress and deportment to tell the world that I needed no one. Because I had been disappointed in love, I believed I would never find a man that shared my interests, understood me, and would let me have my career without competing with me, or worse yet, trying to control me. I had also decided I would have no children because I would not be a good mother. It is interesting to look back on it now and see that everything I believed contradicted the way I had been raised, in a loving Eastern Orthodox Christian home and church community. My father's family emigrated from Glina, a small Serbian village in the former Yugoslavia, and my mother's family came from the city of Mytilene on the Greek island of Lesvos. Baptized at six weeks in the Holy Resurrection Serbian Eastern Orthodox Church in Steubenville, Ohio, I attended that church for most of my first eighteen years.

As I gazed around the classroom, I found myself attracted to a young man who had been sitting quietly before class started. It is odd that I gave him a second look at all because he was definitely not my type. But when the first language drills began, this young man, who said his name was Duane Johnson, called on me asking my name. I blushed and stammered a response. From that moment, we felt drawn to one another. An unmistakable feeling that God desired us to marry grew in each of us before we had a single date. Our first date, on February 4, consisted of a cup of coffee at a local pancake house that lasted nearly until dawn. I learned much that night. Most surprising was that Duane had just finished serving a four-year tour in the Army in Berlin and had decided that he wanted to become Orthodox a month before we met.

Duane was received into the Church. We married the next February. Three years later, on the anniversary of our first date, our beloved son was born. Duane and I had completed our Master of Arts degrees in 1985 and immediately began our doctoral programs. We later had a change of heart, deciding that we wanted children above all else. Thus began the great job search, and I became pregnant while still in graduate school. Duane sold knives door-to-door and worked until midnight at a local restaurant to pay for the doctor's bills because, as students, we had no medical coverage. Just when things looked grim financially, I was offered a job in the Washington area, pregnancy and all. Our families arrived to help us with our move, just as they have always been there for every major event in our lives.

The prospect of moving to the Washington area thrilled all of us. My parents had lived in Baltimore for a number of years after my father finished his tour of duty with the navy. I spent my first few years growing up in Baltimore, and in a way this new job was a homecoming. Duane faced stiff competition for even the lowest-paying job. Many people turned him away as overqualified. One month after we moved, Duane found a job packing boxes in an electronics warehouse.

After what seemed like an entire lifetime of waiting, one morning my water broke. Andrew tried to be born feet first. After sixteen hours of labor, the doctor ordered a Caesarean delivery. Minutes later they lifted Andrew from me and declared, "You have a son!" He cried the squall of a healthy newborn. We were in awe of him and of God, who had given him to us. Andrew Stanar Johnson rested comfortably his first day in the hospital, mostly because of the epidural I received before his delivery. At first the nurses called him "the sleeping one" because he slept so long. When he awoke, they gave him a new nickname, calling him "the wise one." He looked alert, peaceful, and filled with understanding.

We took our son home from the hospital to an apartment filled with flowers and congratulations cards and packages. My mother had cleaned the house and had dinner cooking in the oven. I carried Andrew back to the nursery. It was decorated with a multitude of beautiful things given to us by family and friends. I had stared at that crib for months wondering how it would feel to lay my baby inside it. As I put Andrew in the crib, panic seized me. I had the feeling that Andrew would not grow to manhood.

My mother and I stood watching Andy sleep, but these feelings overcame me. I burst into tears. "Is he really here? Is he safe?" I cried aloud. My mother comforted me. I stopped crying but could not be consoled. Duane did not say a word, and I did not ask him what he thought about my outburst until we started writing this book. When I did ask, Duane told me that what happened in the nursery that morning haunted him for years. At that moment, he understood that I knew something he did not want to know.

2

God Made Everything Beautiful

After that first premonition about Andrew, our lives took the shape familiar to all parents of newborns. We paced the floor with him day and night because it was not unusual for him to be awake for twelve to sixteen hours at a time. Yet we were renewed each day by the wonder of this beautiful child in our lives. At six weeks, Andrew Stanar Johnson was baptized at the Serbian Orthodox Church in Steubenville where I had been baptized and Duane and I had been married. Andrew's first name was his maternal Greek grandfather's middle name and Stanar was for my father's family. His three-part name united his family's Orthodox heritage.

Andrew's first years spun by us at a whirlwind pace. In the midst of baby bottles, chronic ear infections, his first steps, and much, much later, his first words, I would sometimes recall the voice that had whispered so gently within me during Andrew's homecoming that my baby would not become a man. During those moments, I pleaded with God to let me keep my son. I never confided a word of this to anyone, lest speaking the words would make the premonition a reality.

Andrew had chronic ear infections and eczema for which we began treatment at the age of six weeks. Perplexed by his constant crying, I took Andy at three months to the doctor for an evaluation. After the examination, the doctor turned to me. "Mrs. Johnson," he said, "I don't know how to tell you this, but Andrew is bored." I was shocked and asked the doctor how a three-month old baby could be bored. He told me that Andrew did not understand that he was only three months old. Andrew's mind was telling him to do things that only an older child could do like crawling, walking, and exploring. The doctor suggested that we show the baby flashcards and introduce him to every object we could imagine. The doctor also said Andrew had followed our entire conversation, watching each of us speak in turn.

Duane and I began introducing Andrew to everything in our home. Eventually Duane began taking Andy outside to see God's creation: birds, flowers, trees, insects, and Duane's special favorites, cats. Near our apartment there was a wooded area and a stream, which allowed Duane to show Andrew small fish and other stream wildlife. Duane says that nature is one of many immediate pathways to God, for that is how he first came to an awareness of God as a child: nature has in it a presence, an indwelling quality or aspect that points toward Him who made it all, and this is what he wanted Andy to feel. Nature was bigger than anything else, and everything—even ourselves—was contained in it. He wanted his son to realize that nature was there because God had made it, that it was deep, wonderful, and, above all, that it was alive.

This loving attention to nature reaped great rewards. Andrew loved all creation, especially ladybugs because Duane always treated finding a ladybug as an extraordinary event. Andy had a beloved insect collection consisting of plastic specimens. He would not collect live bugs as many children did. On summer evenings, he would spot fireflies from the balcony of our apartment, then run for his jar. When he was fast and lucky enough to catch one, he would put it gently into the jar for a few minutes to admire it and then set it free. One day he came home from preschool with a Japanese beetle that he had captured on the playground. He had convinced the teacher to give him a jar with some grass in it for his new friend. Andy and his guest ate dinner together that evening on his picnic table. He kept that beetle with him every waking moment. The next morning he announced sadly that he was taking the beetle back to school so that it could be with its family. Andy's teacher, Miss Della, took him outside to set the beetle free. That night at bedtime I convinced Andrew to let me tell him a story instead of reading one to him, and the story of "Andy and the Beetle" was born.

"Once upon a time, a little Japanese beetle was playing outside, and he met a boy named Andy. Andy loved the beetle so much that he put him in a jar and took him home to share everything he owned. The beetle ate dinner with Andy, watched Andy take a bath, and slept in Andy's room that night. But the next morning Andy took the beetle back to his mother and father, brothers and sisters. The beetle was happy to have been Andy's friend, and happy that he was back with his family. Each night at bedtime the beetle would gather his brothers and sisters around him and tell them of the marvelous things he saw in Andy's house and what a great friend Andy had been. And as soon as the beetle would finish telling the story, one of his brothers or sisters would plead—'tell us the story again.'" And so would Andrew.

From a very early age, he loved books and stories. Yet, for such a bright infant, Andrew seemed a dumb toddler, in the sense that he did not speak a word. Although he crawled, walked, and did everything else early, at two years of age, he still had no significant speech. No "mama" no "dada". He would only cry for what it was he wanted. Off to the doctor I went again, worried that all the ear infections had affected Andrew's speech and hearing. Again, after extensive examinations, the doctor said, "Andrew understands everything we are saying. He will talk when he wants to talk."

A few months later, Andrew and I stood at the balcony of our apartment looking out of the sliding glass doors. He turned to me. "Birdie is flying," he said softly. I could not believe my ears! His first words. Within a few months we were having complete conversations with Andrew. He had been storing up his words until he could speak complete sentences. As he stored information, he formed many questions. He had also learned all the profanity that I had vowed to give up once he started talking. To my utter humiliation, he knew when and where to use those words. To make matters even more difficult, he could swear in three languages and did so. The questions Andrew had begun to think about in these toddler years were often those prompted by typical childhood curiosity. Others were tinged with a wisdom which made me shudder.

Andrew and I would have many conversations in the car on the way to daycare or home for the evening and while running errands. It was a quiet time alone in the car, and he treasured having me to himself. One morning when Andy was about three, I noticed him looking at his body: two arms, two legs, two hands. "Why don't I have two heads?" he asked. I told him that man had been formed in the image and likeness of God and that he didn't have two heads because God did not create him with two heads. Andrew liked the idea that God had created us, and marveled at the wonderful colors he had used to "paint us."

I remember being particularly exhausted one morning. I turned the car radio on to listen to the news, hoping that Andy would be still and not ask his usual barrage of questions. He listened to the news report along with me, and then asked, "What is a country?" I explained that countries were divided according to geography, language, or the ethnic origin of the people. Then he fixed me with a steady gaze and asked, "Why aren't we one nation?" My heart quickened in my chest as I realized that this question came from the depth of his spirit. I was silent.

I remember another conversation. While driving home one evening. Andrew and I saw a beautiful sunset. "Andy, " I said, "Look at this beautiful sunset God made for us!" He said, "God made it for us?" "Of course he did," I said, thinking the matter was closed, "God made everything beautiful." Andrew thought for a moment. "Did He make the mall?" That question unsettled me. Did my behavior at the mall make Andy think it was something holy? I decided it was time to find a church. One might think that because we spoke of God lovingly and often that we attended church regularly, but we did not. Our move to Maryland was followed closely by the birth of our son. We allowed the stresses of everyday life to convince us that it was too much trouble to get to church on Sunday, particularly since we had to drive forty-five minutes, or more, to the nearest Serbian church.

Although we had not been attending church regularly, our spiritual lives began increasing. This was, in part, because Andrew brought us great healing. When Andrew was born, I weighed over three hundred pounds. I had allowed my perfectionism to nearly ruin my life. No one could live up to my high expectations, not even myself, and nothing was ever enough for me, until Andrew. For him, I wanted to live well. I began to eat healthy foods and to exercise, and I lost eighty pounds. I wanted to be there for him. He loved me so much that I began to love myself more. He always thought I was beautiful, and funny, and loving. I couldn't really see those things in myself, but I began to believe the love I saw reflected in his eyes. Eventually, I all but stopped calling Andrew by his name. I called him Love. At first it puzzled me. I sounded like a bad British movie, "Yes, Love. No, Love. What is it, Love?" But nothing felt better than to address him as what I knew him to be: Love.

Andrew spread his love to all the members of our family, making every gathering a spectacular event, especially the holidays. At dinner, my father would lead our prayers and say a special blessing for our family and those who had departed. We would then gather in a circle around the blessed bread, which had a coin hidden inside. At my father's command, we would each pull a piece of the bread. The person who received the coin was said to be specially blessed that year. Andy looked forward to the time when he would get the coin. He received the coin at Christmas, just two months before his death. He took that coin he treasured and taped it to the icon of Jesus in his bedroom. I have often wondered how his death could be seen as a "special blessing." We are only beginning to understand its meaning.

3

We Find A Spiritual Home

We began, in the next few months, discussing our need to find a church and attend regularly. A difficult decision for our future lay ahead. Duane had finally found a job in his field, after a three-year search, thanks to a friend who recommended Duane to his employers. With the extra income from Duane's new job and my recent promotion, we could either buy a house or have another child. I was nearly thirty-seven years old. We could not wait much longer if we planned to have any more children. But we also desperately longed for our own home, something that with our student loan payments, child care expenses, and the cost of living in the Baltimore-Washington area, had been beyond our reach. We decided the house could wait.

I became pregnant one month after our decision. My happiness gave way to anxiety, however, when I did not have the nausea that I experienced with Andrew. A sonogram at eight weeks showed two sacks, possibly twins! We could see the first fetus, but the second was shrouded in shadow. The news of twins left us in shock. We alternated between excitement and worry. How could we afford twins? We speculated that one of us would have to stop working. Soon our feelings of anxiousness gave way to welcome for the unexpected. My joy ended abruptly one night when I awoke from a dream in which I lost my children in a miscarriage. I cried and made a doctor's appointment. I told the doctor that something was wrong and asked him to run some tests. He spoke condescendingly to me, saying that I was too pretty to cry. I went home angry and filled with fear. I dreamed about my miscarriage again.

The next morning, I called a friend to tell her that something was wrong. She tried to reassure me by saying that every pregnancy is different and that I would not necessarily feel the same way that I had felt when carrying Andrew. She told me to relax. I tried, but that day I began bleeding while on the exercise bike at the gym. I had maintained my eighty pound weight loss. I did not want to zoom up the scale during my pregnancy. I continued counting fat grams even after I knew I was pregnant, and rode the stationary bike with the permission of the doctor, during the first eleven weeks of pregnancy. When I began bleeding, the doctor ordered complete bedrest. I was at home alone when my miscarriage began. I started cramping and bled profusely. My husband was an hour away at work. I could not think clearly. Instead of calling anyone to help me, I phoned the doctor myself. The nurse asked me to drive to a hospital in a distant and unfamiliar area because the doctors who were on duty were there. She did not want to call anyone else in to see me. I agreed, and walked out of my apartment without my car or house keys. I stood bleeding and crying in the hall. A neighbor allowed me to use his phone to call the maintenance man so that I might retrieve my keys.

I climbed into the car, crying, and drove, for what turned out to be a forty-five minute trip. Near the end, I started to become very faint, and for a moment feared for my life. I realized that I should not have been driving. My husband didn't even know what was happening to me or where I was. I could only think that I had to get there quickly to save the babies. When I arrived in the emergency room, I was covered with blood and sobbing. I walked to the admissions room and tried to sit down, but the attendant yelled, "Don't sit there! You'll mess everything up. Wait until I get a sheet!" I was shaking and asked to use the phone to call my husband. They coldly directed me to a pay phone in the hall. I called Duane and told him I was having a miscarriage. "How do you know that?" he asked. I said I was at the hospital with blood pouring down my legs and that I was having contractions. He said he would find directions to the hospital and get there immediately.

A nurse handed me a hospital gown and asked me to undress myself. As I peeled off my bloody clothes, fetal tissue began falling onto the floor. I screamed, "Somebody, please help me!" The nurse ordered an attendant to scoop the tissue off the floor to take it to the laboratory. I asked for my doctor and asked for relief from my pain. But the doctors were in a hysterectomy surgery and could not come. No one would tell me whether I had lost both children.

Duane cried as he held me in the hospital bed. He was afraid he was losing me. Together we waited, mostly in silence, for the doctor to arrive. He told us that we had lost both babies, and he would have to do a D and C. I became hysterical. They had to anesthetize me in order to do the D and C, a procedure that took fifteen minutes. I then began my journey through loss. I opened my eyes and spoke the words "I lost my babies" to the recovery room nurse. She said that I was young and could have other children. She was trying to tell me that everything would be fine. I could not really hear her. All I could feel was a great emptiness, and the feeling of being punished—punished for trying to maintain a reduced-fat diet, punished for not being immediately happy about having twins, punished for every sick and sinful thing that I had ever done. I awoke in hell and wondered what I would tell my son.

Andrew was able to accept the loss with great compassion for me. He looked at the various bandages I wore where I had been poked with needles. He kissed them. I laid on the living room couch with a blanket. He comforted me. Everything in the world was a reminder of what we had lost. Pregnant women were everywhere. Commercials on television were all about babies. I felt hopeless. I called family, friends, and coworkers to tell them of the loss. For the first few days, I sounded as though I could handle things. I said things like, "It's probably for the best. Better now than later" and all those rationalizations we use to hide from our true feelings. After two days, I could no longer look at the blood stains on the carpet and bedspread. I packed up my things, called the office and took a week off from work. I had to go home to heal, to my parents. There we celebrated our family feastday of St. George[1] and then returned to Maryland.

I knew then I could not go on alone. With life-impeding pain as our motivation, we sought out a nearby church, the Orthodox Church of St. Matthew in Columbia, Maryland, which is part of the Orthodox Church in America.[2] In striking contrast to the large, ornate churches of

---

1 In the Serbian Orthodox tradition, it is customary for each family to have an annual Slava, the celebration connected with the day on which a particular saint is commemorated. This day is deemed to be the day on which the family embraced the Orthodox Christian faith.

2 An Orthodox Christian jurisdiction in North America which was granted autocephaly (i.e., self-governing status) by the Patriarchate of Moscow in 1970. It is currently headed by His Beatitude, Metropolitan Theodosius.

my childhood with parishes of five hundred families or more, St. Matthew's is a mission parish, small in size, with no building of its own. The church rented space to worship in a local community center. Each Sunday, parishioners arrive early to set up folding chairs and to bring in an altar and two icons from a closet. On the right side of the altar area, they place the icon of Jesus. The icon of the Holy Virgin Mary with the infant Jesus is placed on the left. I was horrified! "This isn't a church," I said to myself, "it's icons on wheels!"

Another difference was in the altar area. Because St. Matthew's is a mission parish with no iconostas[3], the altar is set up in an open space between the two portable icons. In most Orthodox churches the altar—the holy of holies—is usually hidden behind the iconostas, or, in the case of many Slavic Orthodox churches, it ends up being completely concealed behind the icon screen and a curtain. With the altar out in the open at St. Matthew's, not only did I begin to see what was going on, but I could hear the prayers that the priest says which are usually inaudible to parishioners. I heard Father Ray Velencia pledging, "I will love you, O Lord, with all my heart and mind and spirit." I promised myself that I would do the same.

By far the most radical difference at St. Matthew's is the diversity of its parishioners. Looking around the room, I saw Orthodox Christians of all origins: American, Greek, Serbian, Romanian, Russian, Bulgarian, Arab and Finnish, worshiping together in English with many more children than I could ever recall seeing gathered for worship. At first, I could not see the beauty in this unity of worship. I did not understand that our spiritual journey is not one toward ethnic tradition and custom but rather a journey of discovering Christ. It makes great sense to worship in one's native language, which for most of us born in America is English. Yet I decided that because the worship was in English at St. Matthew's, I would not return. Maybe I thought God didn't speak English. The liturgy sounded strange and harsh to my ears, unlike the melodic and prayerful sound of the Old Church Slavonic[4] that was so familiar to me.

3 A partition usually made of wood and on which icons are arranged. It serves to unite the sanctuary (altar area) with the nave in an Orthodox church.
4 The Slavic language which had its origins in the Bible translation of the 8th century missionaries Cyril and Methodius. It became the standard liturgical

And, as if worshiping in English were not enough of a shock for me, when it was time to partake of the Holy Eucharist, the entire congregation came forward to receive communion! I had never seen anything like it before. As children, we prepared ourselves for communion twice a year by fasting for a week from meat and dairy products and by receiving the sacrament of confession. It was then and only then that we received communion. During our first visit to St. Matthew's, we did not go forward for communion. It was after church that Father Ray explained that frequent communion is the standard in the Orthodox Church in America because it recognizes that the whole point of the liturgy is the Eucharist. When the community gathers together in worship, it should partake of communion as was the case in ancient Christian practice. I did not listen to him and had no plans to return.

During his concluding remarks after the liturgy[5] Father Ray welcomed us by name and invited us to stay for coffee hour. We knew what that usually meant. Everyone would be involved in their own conversations and activities. We would stand around awkwardly for a few minutes, at which time the priest's wife might talk with us. We would then bolt for the door. We agreed to stay. To our surprise, nearly everyone in the church welcomed us and asked if we needed any help, how long we had been in the Columbia community, our son's age, and so on. They were so loving, kind, and helpful that Duane and I became suspicious. They were too nice. Something must be wrong with them.

Duane liked the church, in spite of my misgivings. He suggested that we give it a try. But too many of the traditions with which I had grown up were threatened. I would not return. Another month of desolation over my miscarriage softened my heart and opened it to change. We returned to St. Matthew's on the day of the annual Church picnic to Andy's delight. He frolicked with the other children and left us to find our way with the adults. A week later we attended the annual Church School outing to the Baltimore Zoo. Fa-

language of several Eastern churches and greatly influenced the development of what are now the modern Slavic tongues of eastern Europe and Russia.
5 The principal Orthodox Christian worship service centered around hearing the Word of God and the celebration of the Eucharist. It is a gathering of the faithful headed by the priest.

ther Ray, dressed in red shorts and a T-shirt, took Andy's hand and that of his son, and he walked and talked them through the zoo. Andy was impressed. He gazed in amazement the following day as Father Ray celebrated the liturgy in his beautiful vestments. Andy asked, "Hey, is that the red man?"

Father Ray had become our spiritual guide. His attitude and behavior reflected the spirit of Christ. It was a personal, and thus overwhelmingly powerful, example. This was also possible, in part, because of the simple, profound messages relayed in Father Ray's homilies. His words spoke straight to our hearts. A deeper understanding of God came to us through the English liturgy. After attending church for thirty-seven years, I finally understood the meaning of the words I had been hearing all my life. Because my married name is Johnson, which is not a traditional Orthodox name, people often ask if I am a convert to the faith. I smile and say the answer is yes and no. Both of my parents are Orthodox. I was baptized at the age of six weeks and raised in the Serbian Orthodox Church. Yet I began a conversion when I married Duane, a serious convert who taught me about the Church Fathers and encouraged me to explore the lives of the saints. I completed my "conversion" at St. Matthew's by praying in English and focusing myself on Orthodoxy, not ethnicity. It is a conversion I will spend each day of my life pursuing.

Attending church regularly helped to keep me functioning at work and home. It did not ease the pain of my miscarriage. I remained inwardly devastated and focused my energy on getting pregnant again as a way of redeeming myself. Each month that I failed to conceive, I felt as though I had miscarried again and that I was somehow being judged and punished anew. My feeling of loss fed my low self-esteem. I began to overeat once again to anesthetize my pain. I blamed myself for the miscarriage because I had been counting fat grams and riding an exercise bicycle. It would never happen again. The first month after the miscarriage, I gained twelve pounds. I steadily gained weight each month after that, adding to my shame.

Three months passed with no conception. I was so depressed by August that my parents became concerned about my emotional state and rented a beach house at Nag's Head, North Carolina, for the entire family. Andy loved the beach. The initial bustle of activity upon arrival, the beauty of the ocean, and the comfortable beach house distracted me for a few days. I enjoyed myself thoroughly. Then my period started, once again dashing all my expectations.

That morning I went outside to the sun deck and sobbed. Inside slept my beautiful boy and my loving husband and family. I could not see the blessings I had because there was that one elusive thing I did not have, a baby growing within me. I suffered through the rest of the vacation. My family suffered in the process. I tried putting on my best face, but it was a hollow mask of unhappiness. In September, I was so depressed that I did not even want to try to conceive on the days I had calculated as my fertile period. Once that opportunity passed, I became frantic, thinking that I could not possibly become pregnant until October. My loss angered me. I turned that anger against myself in the form of self-loathing.

The trauma of grief left me physically exhausted. One night, drained of all energy, I lay down sobbing for my babies, eventually crying myself to sleep. That night, I saw my spirit partially lift from my body, staying attached at the stomach, saying, "Sandy, you can be happy now. You are pregnant." I awoke, startled. My body felt as though it were on fire. I dared not hope it was true. The next morning I told myself that I had invented the dream because I was pathetic and lost.

I told my husband and a friend at work about the vision and wanted to take a pregnancy test immediately. Both my husband and my friend advised me to wait, but I went home from work and took the test. I was pregnant. Without the vision, I would not have discovered the pregnancy for another two weeks. I did not feel the surge of joy that I would have expected upon conception. Instead, I felt a stillness and gratitude to God. Standing there in the bathroom, looking at the positive pregnancy test, we decided that this child would bear a special name, a holy one, so that whenever we spoke it, we would remember God's grace and love. In our search we consulted a names book and, once we knew that our baby was to be a girl, we decided to call her Ariana, which is a variation of the Greek name Ariadne, meaning 'blessed by God'.

Four months passed, enough time to preclude the possibility of another early miscarriage, before we gathered enough courage to tell Andrew about my pregnancy. He had not been able to understand the concept of "losing" a baby. Every time he would see an infant at the grocery store, he would ask me if that was the baby I had lost. Andy seemed happy knowing that we were going to have a baby again. His incessant questions began anew beginning with the process of conception. He studied my stomach. "Mommy, how did that baby get in there?" Fortunately, I had already done some thinking about this and had talked to my husband and with a friend a work. My friend advised me to tell Andrew the correct anatomical parts and how they are used to reproduce. She pointed out that this avoided any shame in naming body parts and gave the children information they needed. But I could not bring myself to tell my five year-old boy what body parts are involved in making a baby. An explanation of our anatomy, in our minds, diminished the essence of life and procreation. I was ready when Andy asked me his question. I told him that Mommy and Daddy loved him and loved each other very much. Because we had love to offer a child, God put a baby in my tummy for us all to love. I walked into Andrew's Kindercare class several days later and two of his friends rushed over to me. "Is it true that you and Andy's Daddy love each other, so God put a baby in your tummy?" a little blond-haired girl asked me. Their eyes were as round as saucers. "Yes," I told them, "it is true." I silently mouthed a prayer of thanks.

The miscarriage cast a shadow of anxiety over my pregnancy. "This time," I told myself, "you are not going to kill your baby by counting fat grams or exercising." So I ate, and ate, and ate out of fear and frustration. At one point I even told my doctor that I was using ice cream as a sedative. He laughed. I guess food is not as immediately life-threatening as alcohol or drugs. But for me, food had become just as addictive as any chemical substance. The months of anticipation ended a few weeks before my due date when I stood up one evening from the easy chair in the living room and my water broke. Andy had been sitting beside me at his little red and yellow plastic picnic table industriously working on a project. The sight of water gushing down my legs amazed him. "Daddy, look," he yelled. "Mommy is peeing on the rug!" The hustle of activity to get to the hospital began. I had explained to Andrew earlier that the baby in my tummy was in a little swimming pool. I told him that the pool was now draining because his sister was ready to come into the world.

My family arrived the next day to celebrate Ariana's birth. Everyone carefully included Andrew in the gift and compliment giving.

Andrew was a proud big brother. He wore a set of Christian Cru-
sader armor and helmet to the hospital, a gift from one of his aunts.
Underneath his armor Andrew wore a T-shirt with a "I'm a Big
Brother" button on it. After a few days, Andy looked at my stomach
again and in his childish innocence asked, "Mom, if you had the
baby, why are you still fat?" The woman in the next bed laughed.
Later that night, I heard her telling someone on the phone about my
son's question. I was humiliated, but I could not blame Andy for his
honesty. He loved me and thought I was beautiful no matter how
my body looked. I tormented myself over his comment. How could
I explain to a child that I ate out of fear? Why could I not just stop?

The family gathered again six weeks later at St. Matthew's for
Ariana's christening. After the baptism, Andy seemed to sprout
wings. He became more independent and mature. I could see my
baby boy disappearing before my eyes. This new little man had ideas
of his own, chief among them was a keen desire to fly. One day I
emerged from the bedroom to find Andrew on his knees. He clasped
his hands in prayer, eyes shut, head bowed. "Please God, let me fly,"
he said. Fear gripped me. Taking a step forward, I intended to stop
him, but I relented. This was between Andy and God. I had no
business interfering.

4

Andrew's Flight to Manhood

Andrew's prayer to fly would be answered in a variety of ways. His first flight was to Kindergarten in August of 1992 where he met and fell in love with his first teacher, Miss Codd. I took the day off from work. We launched his new venture with a pancake breakfast at a local restaurant. Andy was excited and ready for an adventure. Asking our waitress to take a picture, we smiled broadly for the camera. Then we returned home to get Andy's colorful new dinosaur backpack. When it was time for the afternoon Kindergarten class to begin, Andy and I set out on foot to Oaklands Elementary School. A few hundred feet outside our door, Andy spotted some other boys and ran off. I watched as he caught up to them and began chattering. I ran as well as I could at my weight trying to catch up to him. As the boys arrived at school, they were greeted by Miss Codd who stood at the head of a line of children waiting to go into the classroom. Andy stopped for a moment with his two new friends to dig around for some bugs. Then he proceeded up the line saying, "Hi, I'm Andy Johnson. What's your name?" Like an old politician running for re-election, he worked his way up the line shaking people's hands. Reaching the head of the line, he looked directly at the teacher and said, "Miss Codd, that's the name of a fish!" And he was ready. I looked at Miss Codd, and then turned to one of the other mothers and said, "That is the woman who is going to be writing me notes all year!"

Miss Codd invited the children to follow her to the classroom, and since Andy was already at the front of the line, he proceeded down the hall. I stood there and watched as his little head disappeared through the schoolhouse door with not so much as a "Goodbye, Mom! See you later." I wondered whether I should go inside or just go home, and I decided to get a picture of him in the classroom. Andy had already seated himself at a little table and chair and was taking off his book bag as I entered. He looked surprised when he saw me, silently asking me what I was doing there. I took his picture, kissed him and departed. At home I wept a few tears for my baby who had grown up so quickly.

Andy loved school and Miss Codd. He said prayers for her every night. She needed them because he drove her absolutely crazy. At school he was a bundle of energy, and he could never do enough. Incessantly engaged in projects, he could outlast anyone's endurance. He was always busy, and there was not much quiet time. Miss Codd had at least twenty other pupils to look after in her class, so she became a little frustrated with Andrew. During our first parent-teacher conference that fall she told me that Andrew was brilliant and creative, but there was a problem. She did not know exactly how to tell me. "Just say it," I urged her.

"He's compulsive," she replied.

I had to laugh. "He comes from a long line of compulsive people, including me, " I confessed. "What is he compulsive about?" She said that he kept doing the projects even after the lesson had been completed.

"The bottom line is that he is trying to cram eight hours of school into a two-and-a-half hour session, and that can be upsetting," she said. I agreed. Andy had a mind and a timetable of his own. He felt like he had to do as much as he could, and that was exactly what he was doing. I did not judge or punish him for his behavior in school. We returned home, and I asked Andy about his behavior at school. He could not think of anything he had done wrong.

His love for Miss Codd continued despite their sparring. One afternoon after school he told me that Miss Codd did not have enough fish magnets. He wanted to give her a tropical fish magnet from the door of our refrigerator, a souvenir of our vacation at the beach. He did. When I picked him up the next day, Miss Codd said, "He's brought me this fish magnet!" She was very surprised. I told her that Andy said she had told the class that she did not have enough fish magnets. Miss Codd did not expect a child to remember and respond to that statement. She tried to give it back, saying she would order some more magnets. I asked her to keep it because Andrew wanted her to have it.

Andy's flight to manhood continued in September of 1992 when he became an altar boy at St. Matthew's at the age of five years.

His early interest in serving was piqued, in part, by the proximity of our seats to the altar, the main icons, and the censer. We usually sat on the left hand side of the church in the second row. If Andy became distracted during the liturgy, we would point out the altar boys to him. He would then watch their preparations and their handling of candles and the censer. When our principal altar boy left with his family in September of 1992 for Texas, Father Ray announced their departure with sadness, for we would miss them. He also called upon the children of the church to think about serving. I turned to Andy following that liturgy and asked him if he thought he was ready to be an altar boy. He said yes. We approached Father Ray that very day during coffee hour and explained that Andy wanted to serve as an altar boy. Father Ray looked somewhat surprised but agreed that we could try. His wife Debbie prepared an altar boy's robe for Andy. He wore it with pride and began serving liturgy the following week. From that moment, he was everything the Lord intended him to be. I think that Father Ray and Debbie described Andy's presence best when they said that there was something "otherworldly" about him. As Andy served with Father Ray, I would often see Father Ray turn and look directly into Andy's eyes, not seeing a child there, but a brother in Christ who appreciated the depth of the worship being celebrated that day.

One of Andrew's greatest joys was being able to receive communion before the rest of the congregation. This love, on one occasion, interrupted what was the customary flow of a chrismation Sunday. A married couple had been received into the Church and they were about to receive their first communion. The husband stepped up to the chalice, but Andrew had decided that it still had to be his turn. He stepped in between Father Ray and the new communicant, lifting his shining face to the chalice. He could not be denied. Father Ray served him.

The pictures of Andrew's first day as an altar boy reflect the genuine pride and joy he felt wearing his robe. He stood in it beaming like the sun bursting through the clouds. He clasped his magic marker-stained fingers together in the prayer of the pure in heart. His pride in being an altar boy led him to suggest that he should be a priest for Halloween. I told him that there was more involved in becoming a priest than putting on a costume and that he would have to choose another costume.

Part of our church activities included taking meals to the homeless, and Andy would always help us carry food into the shelter. He
could not understand why people were homeless. Often when he saw
people walking alone alongside the road, he would ask why they were
not in their cars. I would explain that not everyone owns a car, or a
home, and that some people were very poor. This saddened him.

At McDonald's, I would give Andy money to put into the Ron-
ald McDonald fund for the care of critically ill children and their
families. After giving money to the McDonald's charity and eating
lunch there one afternoon, we went to get groceries. Up and down
the aisles we walked, gathering our food for the week. Andy then
asked, "Where is the food for the poor?" He wanted to put money
into a collection box. There was nothing of that sort available at the
grocery store at that time. I told Andy that a grocery store was a business that was not necessarily interested in feeding the poor. How I
regretted those words! After that, he would refuse to go to the store
with me. He demanded that I stop buying my food from people who
did not care about the poor.

Occasionally, this boyish truthfulness would overshadow his
concern for others. Those instances became learning opportunities
for us both. As we shopped one day at a discount store, I carried an
armload of items, one or two of which were treats for Andrew. He
noticed a large woman coming toward us and exclaimed gleefully,
"Look, mama, she is fatter than you are!" The woman heard him,
and her face crumpled in shame. I dropped all my items onto the
nearest table and marched Andrew outside. "Don't you ever say anything like that again!" I looked directly into his eyes and forcefully
continued. "When you see someone who is ugly, fat, crippled, or
otherwise different than you, you must love them. Love is what they
need, not you pointing out what is wrong with them!" He agreed.
We left without buying anything.

Andy did not cry or protest over this lesson. Many months later
I learned just how seriously he took my words, and I regretted that I
was so harsh with him that day. Sitting in a restaurant with Andrew
and some of our friends, we noticed one of the St. Matthew's parishioners eating at another table. She had had a brain tumor and recent
surgery to treat it and, as a result, her hair was gone. She wore a scarf
around her head, and we chatted briefly with her and went back to

our dinners. It was during the next few days that Andrew would say, "Mom, I have something to tell you, but I can't." I assured him that he could tell me anything. "I can't tell you this," he said, and this conversation would repeat itself. It really bothered me that he could not tell me something. I wondered why. Finally, he confessed to his father that he had noticed that our friend from church did not have any hair and that he wanted her to get it back. Duane explained to him that her illness was the reason for her appearance and that indeed her hair would grow back in time. He had been afraid to tell me, lest I launch into him again for pointing out a person's physical problem. I assured him that his hope for our friend's hair growing back was not a hurtful thing.

On another occasion, Andrew and I had walked to a local convenience store. I bought him ice cream, and we started to walk home. Passing the playground near our apartment, we heard a child crying. A young child sat alone at a picnic table, her head buried in her hands sobbing. We sat beside her. I asked her what was troubling her. She said her stepmother hated her. We did not know this child or her parents. I assured her that she was loved and that, even though parents sometimes become angry, that does not mean you are not loved. She stopped crying and sniffled. Andy handed her his ice cream. We sat quietly for a while, and her sister appeared to take her in to dinner.

It was at this same playground in October that an older child approached Andy and asked to borrow his bike. Andrew had gone to the playground alone, a very new privilege for our schoolboy. He stopped riding his bike in order to play with the other children. It was his first and only bike, which Duane had taught him to ride without training wheels. They were both very proud. Even though he was delighted with his new skill, it had made me a little sad to see my boy flying away from me.

Andy permitted the child to ride his bike. The boy rode away with all his might. Duane happened to see the child riding by our apartment on Andy's bike and took Ariana to the playground to see what had happened In tears, Andy told of the boy who had "borrowed" his bicycle. Duane explained that the bicycle had been stolen. They got into the car and drove around the immediate neighborhood for an hour, looking for the bike and asking children about its whereabouts. Duane was convinced that he would be able to recover the bicycle. He spent the next week looking for it. Every night after work he would swing by one neighborhood in particular. It was not a neighborhood near us, and I could not understand why Duane thought the bike was there. He explained to me that it was the most likely neighborhood, given the direction in which the young thief was headed when he saw him speeding away. I wanted to buy Andy another bike. Duane insisted that the stolen bike was the one Andy had learned to ride. He had to have that bike back. Just when I was just about to buy another bicycle, Duane came home from work one night triumphantly carrying Andrew's bike. His intuition had been right. Duane had once again driven through the neighborhood that he had been searching and finally saw a child riding Andrew's bike. He told the child that it belonged to his son and that it had been stolen.

Andy was overjoyed. I immediately praised Duane for his success and determination. I dialed my parents' phone number so they could hear the great news. They had been distressed that their grandson had been a crime victim. Then Andy took the phone and told them exactly what had happened. "God put a picture of where my bike was in Daddy's head. He went and got it!" Andy saw everything that happened in his life in relation to God. He had eczema; he asked me why God had made him "itchy." He would also on occasion refuse to excuse himself for burping. "God made me that way, didn't he?" was the typical argument. Then he would walk away.

With the bike found, we began to prepare for a happy Halloween. Although I had convinced Andy that he should dress up to be something other than a priest, he did not have any immediate ideas, other than what was by then the predictable need to be a Ninja Turtle. I decided that he would be a mummy. I made Andy's costume out of strips from an old faded sheet, which I sewed to his thermal underwear. I worked past midnight for several nights before Halloween. It is true that I am not much of a seamstress, and Andy grew tired of being my Halloween experiment. Finally, he asked me one night in complete exasperation, "Oh, why couldn't I have just been a vampire?"

When his costume was finished, he was thrilled. I gave him an Egyptian necklace featuring a mummy and two scarabs to wear as the mummy's amulet. Now it grieves me that I made him something

dead on his last Halloween. Duane says that it is just one more example of the little things that just keep adding up about Andy's
death. Of all the things that Andy could have been on that last Halloween, he was a mummy. Duane pointed out that even though the
mummy is a dead body, it is also a body that has been prepared to receive the divine gift of eternal life.

We know that Andrew was aware of this divine gift and looked
forward to it. He had a relationship with Christ that we cannot describe. We do not know the exact nature of this relationship because
it frightened us. Andrew would sometimes make statements that we
could have explored further by asking him questions. Instead, we
took these statements at face value because we were not ready to hear
anything more. The most vivid memory that I have of this type of
exchange was when I went to the grocery store with Andy and Ariana after work one day. I needed to buy food and cook dinner before
Duane got home from work. The parking lot was the typical rush-
hour frenzy. I waited for several minutes for a parking spot close to
the store. Someone in another car jumped ahead and took that
space. I cursed them. Andrew drew himself up in his seat. "God
doesn't like it when you talk like that," he said. I became even more
angry. I had enough problems without my five-year-old son preaching to me. So I snarled, "How do you know?" Andy turned his shining face slowly to me, looked me squarely in the eye and with great
peace and purpose said, "He told me." Fear kicked into my stomach,
not just at Andy's words but at the look on his face. I became silent,
afraid to ask him anything else.

As I mentioned before, many of our significant conversations
took place when we were together in that car. Another fall day as we
were coming home from daycare, Andrew turned to me and asked,
"Mom, what happens when you are in a car accident?" Imagining
that he was thinking of a fender-bender, I told him that the cars pull
to the side of the road and exchange insurance information. "But
what happens if you are hurt," he pressed. I told him an ambulance
takes you to the hospital and makes you all better. "Where do they
take you if you are already dead," he asked quietly, his chin resting
cupped in his hands and staring straight ahead out the window.

This was all I could bear. Fear flashed through me. I began
screaming at him, nearly hitting the car in front of me. "Where do

you get things like this?" I asked. "I'm not even going to discuss this!" He told me he was sorry. He took apologies very seriously and would sometimes remember for weeks or months when he had offended someone. For instance, that fall the president of the PTA had rebuked him when she caught him and her grandson playing in a stream. The stream is a potentially dangerous area that is forbidden to the school children. Andrew, more than a month later, upon seeing her at school, hung his head and asked if she were still angry with him. She reassured him, saying that she had never been angry and was only concerned for their safety. He went away happy and satisfied. She said she had never seen anything like it in a child. On another occasion, Andy dropped the censer during church, causing a flurry in the middle of liturgy as people scrambled to clean up the red-hot coals and scattered ash. After church, he stood outside the door waiting for Father Ray to take off his vestments. He apologized when Father Ray emerged. Father Ray told us that Andy's spirit could not rest until he made sure that there were no hard feelings.

5

Homeward Bound

A ndy's identity in Christ continued to deepen during the winter of 1992. The annual church school play took place on the St. Matthew's parish feast day in November. Andrew was assigned the part of St. Stephen, one of the Church's first deacons and its first martyr. I rehearsed his lines with him every night, urging him to speak clearly and distinctly. We dressed him in an old beige and white striped robe of mine and put a kaffiyah on his head. He was ready for the part.

On the day of the play, he was the star of the show. He spoke his lines clearly and with conviction. He began by saying, "Justin and I have been going from city to city giving money to poor people." In the play, he was addressed by a woman seeking healing for her arm. He faced her asking, "Do you believe in Jesus? Do you believe His power can make you better?" The woman said that she did believe in Jesus. Andy responded, "Then in His name and by His power, I bless you to make you better." The townspeople decide that he has blasphemed. He is to be stoned to death. He then asked God to forgive the people who were about to kill him, saying "Father forgive them. I see Jesus sitting at the right hand of God." And as the people began to stone Andy, he delivered his last line. "Into your hands, I commend my spirit." In his best theatrical style, unplanned and unrehearsed, he stuck out his tongue in imitation of death and fell face forward. The audience roared with laughter and approval. Andy had given quite a performance, which our parish historian, captured on film. It is ironic that it is the only videotape I have. On this tape my son commends himself to God and dies, a short three months before his own death.

Ana, a blind octogenarian member of the parish sent for me after the performance. "Sandy," she said. "I take back everything I thought and said about Andy being too young to be an altar boy. I could hear him in that play, and he really understood and believed what he was saying. He is quite an extraordinary child." She was right about one thing, Andy understood and believed what he was saying. He spread the word of Jesus on and off stage. He took his earthly ministry so seriously that it cost us a beloved daycare provider in January.

After Ariana's birth, we began searching for a daycare provider who would keep both children. We needed someone in the neighborhood who could walk Andy to afternoon kindergarten classes. One afternoon at the playground, I confided my problems to one of our neighbors. She was a devout Pakistani Muslim, who said if I couldn't find anyone else, she would be willing to take my children. This family did not need the money. Her husband operated his own pharmacy; they owned a Mercedes. But she loved children and had a three-year-old of her own at home. She also watched another neighbor's son. Dressed in traditional Pakistani garb, they were a close-knit family unit, who prayed together five times a day as is prescribed in Islam. No alcohol, no tobacco, and they sought God. We could not think of a better situation. We took our children there.

Our families soon became very close. We traded food recipes and attended each other's birthday parties. Each time we entered their home, they made us the guests of honor. At one of these parties, the birthday girl proudly showed Andrew a gold bracelet with a few semi-precious stones in it that she had received as a gift from a relative in Pakistan. He thought it was beautiful and immediately exclaimed, "Can I have that for my mom?"

But one day in January our sitter approached me and looked troubled. She said, "My husband wants me to work at his business. I will no longer be able to care for your children." Not knowing what to think, I told her how sorry I was and left. At home, I cried. What would we do now? Why would our sitter do this to us?

I knew that it was extremely unlikely that she would be going to work. My hunch was validated when I called the family of the other child that she watched and discovered that they were not asked to find another sitter. Racking our brains for an answer, we could not find one because we knew they loved our children. We thought perhaps she had tired of taking Andy to kindergarten in the afternoon or that the boys had become too loud. But we got our answer the following Sunday after church when we stopped at the video store to get a video for Andy and me to watch that night. Duane was going to see Bishop Kallistos Ware give a talk on Orthodoxy and, as the talk was in the evening and too late to keep the children out we were going to have a special evening of our own at home. Andy asked why Daddy was going to hear the bishop. "Daddy loves God," I answered, "so he wants to hear everything about God." We were taking the children out of the carseats. Andy responded, "That's what I tried to tell Assad!" Duane and I jerked our heads up and looked at each other. "I told him you have to love God. Assad doesn't even know who Jesus is. I told him Jesus died for our sins, and you have to love God." We now had our answer. The sitter had quit because Andy was preaching Christianity to her children, a crime punishable by death in the stricter Muslim countries. I looked at Andy. "When did you tell Assad this, Andrew?" Spreading apart his hands in exasperation, he answered, "Every day!"

The sitter dropped by unexpectedly several days later to bring some things the children had left at her home. She stopped in front of a picture of Andrew in his altar boy's robe that was sitting on our china cabinet. "He's an altar boy at our church," I explained. She cut me off. "Believe me, I know all about it," she said.

In January, Ariana's godmother Joy helped me find another sitter who lived close to school. The new sitter was loving and licensed. Andrew, Ariana, and I visited with her several times before the actual day on which I planned to leave them in her care. While the children were playing during our second visit, I noticed that Andrew seemed to be fading from sight. To me, he did not look like the other children playing there. They looked fixed and permanent, made of flesh and blood. Andrew seemed made of spirit that was departing. I panicked inwardly. We watched the children play for another thirty minutes. Then I bundled them up warmly and headed home. When I got there, I sat immobilized in our old easy chair, fear pumping through my veins. Duane asked me what was wrong. I burst into tears. "Andy's not like those other little boys he was playing with." "What do you mean," Duane asked. I didn't know how to answer without expressing my fears, which were inexpressible. "He's so fragile," I sobbed. "Fragile?" Duane looked at him romping around the living room. "What do you mean, he's fragile?" I had no answer for him. I continued crying.

Then the dreams about Ariana began. They were terrifying dreams in which Ariana lay in a crib in a pediatric intensive care unit, with tubes coming out of her wrists. A voice quietly spoke to me, "She survives." I awoke frightened, and later told my husband about the dream. I had the same dream a few weeks later. I watched her closely, feeling helpless.

Soon it was the fourth of February, Andy's birthday, which was always celebrated with multiple parties: in school, a pizza party at the local "Chuck E. Cheese" children's playland, and at home. I took the day off work for his birthday as I did every year. My mother came to celebrate with us as was her custom. Andy and I decorated cupcakes to take to school. I had chocolate icing and little candy cars to put on top of the cupcakes. I would spread the icing, and Andy arranged the car decorations. I noticed that he began standing them up straight on their hoods instead of laying them down flat. You couldn't even recognize that it was a car standing in the air, so I asked him what he was doing. "This is where Jesus and the two others died," he said.

A week later he was in his room playing with cars while Duane and I made dinner. Andy approached me. "Do I really have a guardian angel?" he asked. "Of course you do, Andy. The day you are baptized, the Lord gives you an angel of your very own." "Does this angel take me to heaven when I die?" "Yes," I answered, beginning to frown. He continued, "What are the rules for getting into heaven?" "You must love God and other people, Andy. You don't have anything to worry about. You've done everything you need to get into heaven." "Oh boy, thanks!" he said spinning on his heel and romping back into the bedroom. Duane and I looked at each other wondering what that was all about. We did not ask.

That same week Duane read Andrew the story of the young prophet Samuel in the Children's Bible that we often read to him at bedtime. It was the account of how God spoke to the boy Samuel and how the priest Eli helped him to understand what was happening. As Duane read this story to Andy, he looked up at his face and saw an enigmatic smile, the expression of a person who hears something that he already knows.

As the third week of February approached, Ariana developed a severe case of flu virus. It began on a Saturday so I stayed home with her the following day while Duane and Andrew went to liturgy. It was during Communion that Andrew, after being the first to partake because of his status as altar boy, would move to the wine and *prosfora*[1] table so that he could officiate there. He liked to stand by in his smart altar boy's robe and replenish the wine cup as needed. On that day Duane and another parishioner stood by to keep an eye on him. It was in the middle of his duty that Andrew turned to Duane and asked, "Daddy, do we really drink *Bozhe*'s[2] blood?" Duane, startled by the question, looked at the other parishioner's raised eyebrows, and then answered, "Yes, Andy, we do." He looked back in the direction of the oncoming communicants, appearing to be satisfied.

That week we had planned to drive to Ohio for the baptism of my sister's infant daughter. It was not possible to travel because of Ariana's illness. I had to work feverishly to ensure that Ariana did not dehydrate. She was going through about twenty-five disposable diapers a day because of the intestinal diarrhea. Duane and I took turns staying home from work with Ariana from Monday through Thursday. On Friday Andrew woke up and vomited. He had never been so happy in his life. Now he got to stay home with Mommy and Ariana, who was at last beginning to feel better. He settled into his pajamas and "dak" (his name for his blanket) and was not sick again all day. Then he began lobbying for all of the things that he wanted to do. He wanted a new "Attack Pack" car, a toy which fascinated him because it was a vehicle that also featured a gaping mouth filled with sharp teeth when you pressed the button. I ran out of diapers. We had to go out anyway, so I agreed that we would get his car. Walking out the door, he turned to me asking, "Mom, are we going to get my car first?" I agreed. "OK! Then can we get lunch from McDonald's?" "I thought you were sick," I said to him. "Oh, I am," he replied, wrinkling up his face, "but I'm still a little bit hungry." We got the diapers, the Attack Pack car, and got him a Happy Meal from the McDonald's drive-thru on the way home. While we were eating lunch, one of my teeth began to splinter. I had had a root canal years earlier, but kept putting off having a crown put on the tooth because it was so expensive. I went into the bathroom and be-

---

1 The bread baked specifically for use in the Orthodox liturgy. A portion of it is set aside and is prepared and consecrated as part of the Holy Eucharist, with the unconsecrated remainder of it being consumed after receiving communion and/or after the conclusion of the liturgy.

2 The Old Church Slavonic word for God's.

gan to cry. Then I thought to myself, "What are you crying about? It's not like you've lost a child."

Saturday was a wonderful day. Andy felt great, and had no signs of illness. We headed off to the movies to see the tale of two dogs and a cat who get separated from their owners and travel across the mountains to get home to them again. He crawled onto my lap when he was frightened by some owls hooting in the night forest. The moment overpowered me. I studied the shape of his little head nestled against me and knew that I would not have many more chances like that. After all, he was six. I thought there would soon come a time when he would not want to sit on my lap. Until I sat down to write this I did not realize the significance of the title of the film we saw that day, Andy's last. The title is "Homeward Bound: The Incredible Adventure."

After Andy's bath that night, he stopped me in the hall, hugged me and declared, "You are the best mommy, and I love you!" He had also told his father the same thing earlier that week. We expressed our love for each other often, but Andy's declaration to us that weekend differed from our usual expressions of love and affection. It struck me as a bit odd because it sounded almost like a little prepared speech. I did not understand and felt unsettled.

On Sunday morning we wanted to be in Ohio with the rest of the family celebrating the christening of our niece. We were disappointed that we could not go. We decided that everyone was well enough to go to church. Outside, snow fell steadily, covering the roads. Joy called to say that their family would not be going to church because the roads might become too bad to get home after the service. I heard Andy telling her that he was the altar boy and was going to church. Looking outside, I began to grow nervous. I stood at the sliding glass doors where Andy and I had watched birds for years, the spot upon which he had spoken his first words as I held him in my arms, and that spot was only inches away from the place near the couch where he had knelt in prayer, begging God to let him fly. I said, "Maybe we should just stay home." No one agreed. Instead, we decided to go out to the main roads to see their condition. The roads looked passable. We could even see some clear patches, so we set off for church. Andrew sat in the back seat behind the driver's position, happily playing with the miniature cars that his godfather George had given him at Christmas.

At one point along the way we stopped at a red light, and Andrew held up a little tow truck, itself holding another small car, and said proudly, "Look Mom! This truck can hold up this car." I smiled at him. He grinned from ear to ear. I turned back around as we moved through the intersection and began to go down a long, gradual grade. It was the very next instant that we hit a patch of ice and the car began to swerve out of control, the rear of the vehicle swinging around in a 180 degree circle as we careened left of center into the oncoming traffic lanes. I looked at my husband, his face frozen in horror as he saw a huge truck approaching us. The truck hit us, twice, and life would never be the same.

6

Life, As We Had Known It, Ends

As we lost control of the car, I did not feel any panic. I had slid off the road before in bad weather, and nothing horrible had ever happened. I was not afraid. But the truck hit at the point where Andrew was sitting, the left rear corner bore the brunt of the impact. The car spun, and the truck hit us again. When the car stopped spinning at the side of the road, I looked at my husband. He was sprawled across the steering wheel, eyes mere slits, blood pouring from his head and mouth. I thought he might be dead. Then I looked in the back seat at the children. Andy was dead. Ariana was unconscious.

I began to scream. "No! No! No!" I grabbed hold of my husband's arm. "I cannot do this alone," I screamed. "Duane, Duane, Duane!" I shrieked his name with every fiber of my being. Then he sat bolt upright, looked at me, and fainted away. Kicking open his car door, I began pushing him out. I reached over the seat and took Ariana out of her carseat and shook her. She began to cry. I handed her to the truck driver who had hit us. People began to gather and begged me not to go back to the car, saying that emergency help was on the way. Blood poured out of a gash in my head. I could feel a continuous warm flow of it on my face and neck. I spat the blood pouring down my face out of my mouth and went back.

I made my way to the back seat of the car and gazed at my son. He was gone, as peacefully as an angel. He looked beautiful. His face held no hint of fear or pain. He had not shed a single tear. Andy had been at the point of impact of the truck. He died instantly. His body was sandwiched into the wreckage so that I could not pull him from the car. The truck had pushed the trunk of the car, like an accordion, into the back seat of the car. We kept Andy's robe in the trunk of the car so that it would not wrinkle on the ride to church. By smashing the trunk into the back seat, the truck joined Andy and his robe at the moment of his death. Andrew's robe became stained with his own blood.

I stared dumbly at his beauty, touched his cool cheek and whispered, "Oh, Andrew," knowing that I was saying goodby. I kissed him. The snow fell in slow motion. I began to scream. "My son, my son! Lord Jesus Christ, please don't take my son." I screamed this over and over. As I stood confronting a cold reality that I knew I could not bear, a part of myself died. I screamed and felt myself falling, falling to a place deep within my soul. The Lord was there to hold me upright. I spoke to Him saying, "For whatever reason this has happened, I know that you have done what is right for my son. I submit to your will."

The emergency crews arrived and led me away from my Andy. They sat me down on the curb and put a neck brace on me and tried to stem the blood flowing from my head. The crew had to chop out the front seat with an ax to get to Andy. As they carried him past me, they told me not to turn my head. I did not. Paramedics placed Andy on a stretcher alongside the car on the side of the road. His shoes had come off when they lifted him out of the car. I saw a little green sock. The rest of his body was obscured by the car. The policeman directing traffic around our vehicle looked down at my son on the stretcher and shook his head slowly back and forth.

Although I knew Andy was dead, I clung to the small hope that, since no one had spoken those words to me, maybe he was still alive. No one dared speak those words to me. Putting me in an ambulance, the attendants cut my coat and clothes off with huge shears. I could hear them saying that I had brain tissue exposed. The two ambulances sped off to the Shock Trauma unit of the Baltimore hospital. Upon arrival at the hospital, doctors and nurses began pulling glass from me. I prayed aloud and continuously. Amid the chaos of doctors and nurses attending me and shaving my head for stitches, a thought floated softly to me. "You must not let this life pass unnoticed. You must write a book." Write a book? I thought in horror! Where was this thought coming from? The thought then became louder and more imperative. "You must not let this life pass unnoticed. You must write a book!" I muttered, "OK, OK"—more to make it stop than anything else.

The doctor asked for my family's phone number. It was 10 a.m. Divine Liturgy was just beginning in Steubenville. I would not have ruined that baptism for anything in the world. Andy was dead. There was nothing anyone could do for us at that moment. Instead, I gave the doctors the phone numbers of Father Ray and of Ariana's godparents, Joy and her husband Duane. Andy was dead. No one would tell me. Perhaps the doctors wanted me to accept it gradually or wanted to wait until someone was there with me. I had been prepared for this for many years. I just wanted to know. Grabbing the hand of the next doctor to enter my room, I pleaded, " Please just tell me. I have to know."

"Andy didn't make it," he said. I was quiet for a moment. Then I began to grieve for my son, crying, screaming, sobbing, and begging him to forgive me.

"Mommy is sorry, Andy. Mommy is sorry." The doctors and nurses cried. Duane slipped in and out of consciousness most of the day. He had a massive concussion, a broken shoulder blade, and assorted cuts and bruises all over his body as I did. His heart had been bruised when he hit the steering wheel, and his heartbeat had become irregular. The doctor told me that even though Duane was unconscious as he was being attended in the emergency room, he was reacting to my screaming and crying. Duane's blood pressure would go up when he heard me. He did not know that Andrew was gone.

That afternoon, Father Ray arrived with Joy and Duane. They had braved the snowstorm to be with us. When Father Ray walked into the room, the doubts and fears that had been overwhelming me burst out. "I wasn't satisfied. I was never satisfied. I wanted more money. I wanted a house, so God took my Andy." "No, Sandy, no," Father Ray said as he hugged me, tears streaming down his face. Joy and Duane hovered nearby. Joy just kept saying over and over again how she wanted to take my pain away from me. We spoke numbly for a while. The doctors came to tell me that Duane had regained consciousness and that I must go and tell him that Andy was gone. Duane was fighting to regain his senses when they pushed my bed into his room. He looked battered and confused. I told him that Ariana was in the infant intensive care. She had a skull fracture but would survive. I described my injuries to him and told him that I would also recover. Then I told him our son had died. He recoiled in surprise and horror, looking as though he had just been hit by a truck, again. He burst into tears. Father Ray gave us a few minutes alone and then had the nurses bring Ariana to us. He gave us communion and holy unction[1] for our healing.

---

1 The ritual anointing of the sick with oil. The Orthodox Church prescribes it in cases of serious illness, injury or imminent death.

By that time it was after 6:00 p.m. I asked Father Ray to call our parents. It was one of the hardest things he ever had to do in his life. My parents each picked up a telephone to speak with him, thinking that he had called to congratulate them on the christening. He told them there had been a terrible accident and that we were at Shock Trauma. As he began describing our injuries, my mother broke in asking, "What about Andy?" He quietly told them that Andy didn't make it. My mother dropped the phone and threw herself to the floor screaming. My sisters came running. After taking the rest of the information from Father Ray, my father told him that they would be on the next flight out to Maryland. Father Ray also called Duane's mother in Ohio to tell her the tragic news. While Father Ray made these difficult phone calls from the hospital, our parish family at St. Matthew's formed a telephone network to inform everyone in the community of Andy's death.

Our visitors departed, and the nurses moved us into separate, private rooms. My parents arrived at 2 a.m. Still awake and crying, I blamed myself and believed that they also blamed me. Why shouldn't they? They had four children and none of us had died. I had not taken care of my child. He was dead, and my mother loved him more than anything else on this earth. I had robbed her, and I believed she would never forgive me. My parents, in shock themselves, reassured me and then went to the infant intensive care to see Ariana. She was in a crib with an IV tube coming out of her wrist, whimpering. When my mother asked her whereabouts, Ariana heard and recognized her voice. Lifting her head from the crib she began to look about for her Baba.[2] My mother held her and rocked her to sleep. Then she and my father went to a hotel. It was that night that Andrew appeared to my mother in a dream. He told her to stop crying. She just cried harder. He stomped his foot and spread his hands, saying, "Don't cry, Baba."

The next morning, the hospital staff took more tests. My head injury was not life-threatening. I was to be released that very day. A young social worker came to interview me. She looked very uncomfortable and asked me an endless stream of questions. I grew tired and finally said, "I am not going to kill myself, if that is what you are asking me. Suicide is against

2 The Serbian word for grandmother.

my religion. If I did kill myself, I would never see my son again." She departed. I was also visited by a priest who had been with the paramedics at the scene of the accident. He assured me that Andy did not suffer and that he had prayed for him and us. The State Patrol officer at the scene also came to express his sympathy. I stared at him and said, "Andy had his seat belt on." I remembered the television commercial in which a police officer says, "I've never unbuckled a dead person." I now knew that it was not true. These strangers were the first of many special people who were touched by our son's death and reached out to us in faith and in love.

A nurse put me in a wheelchair and took me to the children's intensive care. With my bruised and battered body, shaved head and bandages, some of the children looked frightened to see me. The nurse then wheeled me to a place that I had visited before in my dreams. It was a section of an infant intensive care unit where stood a crib with tall bars. Amid all the tubes, wires and monitoring equipment was my daughter. I held her, but I could not feel anything. She was alive. That was all I could register at that moment. I sat dumbly.

My parents arrived at the hospital that morning, and the sight of them filled me with hope. I could live. They loved me. Here they were again, as they had been at every point in my life, offering love and support, trying to help me to make the best of my life. But there was something in me that hated myself and everyone around me. I felt cold. My father suggested that the doctor should prescribe sedatives for me before my release. I refused any drugs. Drugs would not bring Andy back to life. Drugs would not change this situation. My dad's concern was about getting me home for the funeral. I could understand his anxiety about my condition, but thanks be to God that I knew at that time that drugs would not help. Our pain is there for a reason.

Then my father did one of the thousand quiet acts that fathers perform to take care of their families. He went to the morgue to identify Andrew's body. He stood in the cold steel environment and looked upon the face of his beloved grandson. He then begged the coroner not to perform an autopsy. The coroner agreed to release Andy's body to the funeral home. Thank you, Dad.

Duane's heart beat had been erratic and needed additional monitoring. He had to stay at the hospital for another day. Ariana also needed to remain because the medical staff feared that her skull fracture would lead to spinal meningitis. After my discharge, my parents put me into their rental car. As soon as it began to move, I vomited. I was not ready to get back into a car and move back into the world. The hospital was a place where reality had been suspended. The time had now come to move on.

Walking through the door of our apartment was pure agony. The world that I left behind there included my son. His presence was everywhere. Crying angrily, I began emptying the medicine cabinets of all the antibiotics, ear plugs, steroid creams and antihistamines that Andy had to take every day for his allergies and eczema. He did not need them now. Then I went into his bedroom. The helium balloons from his birthday party that declared "I'm Six" still bobbed about the ceiling. I could not bear it. I took a knife and punctured each of those balloons, stuffing them into the trash. And then I was alone in a room that had once been so filled with love. It was now empty, a vast gaping emptiness that I thought could never be filled.

We had intended, not thinking clearly, to fly straight to Ohio for the funeral and bury Andy at home. We chose to bury him there because we were not sure where our lives would lead us. Father Ray suggested that we have at least one viewing in Maryland so that our church family, friends and coworkers could bid farewell to Andrew. We agreed, and called the funeral home on Monday. We planned to have one evening service in Maryland, then fly Andy home to Ohio for his funeral and burial. He had prayed to fly. I never thought it would be like this. I chose Andy's clothes and asked Father Ray to find another altar boy's robe in which to bury Andy since Andy's was stained with his blood from the accident. Father Ray had anticipated my wish and brought me another one to use. I chose the clothes that Andy would wear under his robe, and began to press them and put them into a bag: his little gold turtleneck shirt to put under the robe, which is white trimmed in gold, and his black dress pants and socks. My mother helped. I remember being really excited to see Andy. I was unaccoustomed to being separated from him for so long.

We then went to the funeral home on Tuesday to make arrangements. I chose a beautiful white child's casket with gold angels at each corner to bear him aloft. I asked to hold Andrew. The funeral director convinced me that I should not see Andrew until his body had been prepared. This was a mistake. A parent must be allowed to hold her child and say good-bye. The funeral director was not certain that they would be able to prepare Andy's body by that night, but by Tuesday afternoon, they told us they could. The St. Matthew's telephone network swung into operation to spread the news of that night's service to those who knew us and our boy. After leaving the funeral home, I began packing for the trip to Ohio. My parents returned to the hospital to get Duane and Ariana. Helping Hands, our church outreach group, brought a meal for us to eat that evening. The doctors reluctantly released Duane and Ariana. Duane was still somewhat disoriented because of the severe concussion and in great pain because of the broken shoulder blade. His speech was also a bit slurred. Concerns about Ariana contracting spinal meningitis continued. The doctors had my mother promise that at the first sign of a fever we would take Ariana to the nearest hospital. Meanwhile, at my parent's home, my aunt and other good Samaritans from the Steubenville church took care of my sisters and helped make arrangements there for Andy's arrival.

The drive to the funeral home in Laurel was quiet and cold. I was still excited just to see Andy. The funeral director escorted Duane and me into the viewing room first to have a few moments alone with our son. Andy's face bespoke of a heavenly peace and love that no funeral attendant could have placed there. We looked at our boy, his fingers still stained with the colored magic markers that he so loved, lying in his casket like a prince. Overwhelmed with love for him, and grief, we were numb. I looked at my husband crying. "He deserves to suffer," I thought to myself. "He was driving the car and killed Andy." That thought crept across me coldly. I wanted to blame somebody. My husband looked at me sobbing and told my mother, "My Sandy, what will she do? She loved him so much."

Others began to gather outside the doors. It was time to begin the service. We sank down into chairs, sobbing. The doors to the room opened. Hundreds of people had come on a moment's notice. One by one they prayed for us and Andrew, saying good-bye. They filed past one at a time to console us, including family, friends, church members, coworkers, Andy's teachers from his elementary school and from Kindercare, the school principal, a cafeteria worker who said she loved the way he smiled at her every day; parents of children with whom Andy had been in daycare, PTA members, neighbors, and our church choir. I told Miss Codd, his kindergarten teacher, that he loved her and remembered her in his prayers each night.

As people filed past us, one member of our church embraced me. He whispered in my ear, "Don't let the Devil tear you apart." I looked into his eyes and knew just as surely as I heard those words that Christ had spoken to me through this person. In that instant, my understanding of evil crystallized. Evil became just as real and vivid as the Lord was to me. Evil had been speaking to me when I thought that my husband deserved to suffer. Upon recognizing that the devil was trying to tear us apart, I felt a flood of compassion and love for my husband. I thought, "How great is his burden. I must help him bear it. I cannot blame him for what is not in his control."

Duane and my mother stood at my sides, my father behind me, until everyone who was able had filed by the casket. Some were too upset even to approach us. The choir began to sing. Father Ray performed the service. His wife Debbie brought a picture of Andy serving. It is my favorite picture. My father looked around the room and told me to never again tell him that we were alone in Maryland. It was filled to capacity, bursting its seams into adjoining halls and other areas. The funeral director said that in all the years they had been in business, they had never witnessed anything like it. The funeral staff itself was affected by Andy's death: it was so upsetting to prepare Andy's body that the four of them had to take turns.

Once again, after everyone departed, Duane and I remained alone with Andy. I stood before him and verbally made a vow. "Andy, Mommy would have died for you a thousand times, but no one gave me that choice. So I promise you now. I will live for you. I will live a life that would have made you proud." I put my head on his chest that was hardened with embalming fluid and sang him his favorite bedtime song, one I had created for him called the "Noodlin' Song." We used to call him "The Noodle" because when he was a baby he had a tuft of hair that stuck up straight on his head like a big noodle. I sang,

> Noodlin', noodlin', mommy's punky noodle.
> Dipsin' and doodlin', mommy's punky noodle.
> My boy, my noodlin' boy.
> Go sleepy bye, baby my boy."

I played with his fingers and gazed at the beloved marker stains. I did not know how I could survive.

7

For Theirs Is the Kingdom of Heaven

The next morning we departed for Ohio. The doctors at Shock Trauma asked us to see our private doctors before we left. Our first stop was at our medical plan building where Duane, Ariana, and I had appointments to be examined. When we walked into that same busy waiting room that we had visited with Andy so many times with ear infections, allergies, and all the other childhood illnesses that kept our faces familiar around the place, I began to sob loudly. Nurses rushed to take us inside, with one shouting, "Get a stretcher! She needs a sedative!"

"Drugs?" I screamed at her, "My son is dead. This is grief. It's normal. Drugs won't help." Anger snapped me back to my senses. We were each seen and released to travel to Ohio for Andy's funeral and burial. The doctors and nurses mourned his passing. Our family doctor spoke reassuringly with us and suggested that upon returning to Maryland we attend a meeting of the Compassionate Friends, an informal fellowship for parents whose children have died.

Everyone piled back into the van for the trip, the first without Andrew. This initiated a long series of "firsts" that I would rather not have endured. In that van, reality once again became suspended. When we reached my parent's home there was no denying that Andy's death was real. The van pulled into my parent's garage. Inside waited my grief-stricken sisters and some other relatives together with a few church helpers. I could not bear to walk through that door without my son. I could not bear to have his death be this real, to see the dazed looks of loss and hurt on the faces of those I loved. So I stayed in the van and would not come out. My father cried as he tried to coax me out of the backseat and into the house. I truly do not know how long it took for me to go inside. When I did, I saw just what I had expected. My sisters looked as though they had been in an accident, too. I felt ashamed and guilty. I blamed myself, thinking, "This is all my fault. I have ruined everyone's lives. Why wasn't I in the backseat instead of him? They say the backseat is the safest place for the children. They say they never unbuckled a dead person! Lies! Lies!"

Everyone tried to comfort us and make us as physically comfortable as possible with our injuries. The next few days remain a blurred agony in our memories. We fell into a pattern that we followed with numb obedience. For two days, we woke up in the morning, went to the funeral home, came home, slept, woke up and went back to the funeral home in the evening. Hundreds of people again came to say good-bye to Andrew and to support our family. Duane and I moved our chairs beside Andy's coffin, so that we could touch him and hold his hands. We sat there for two days holding onto him for our lives. People approached us in horror. I watched my father, knowing that he was shattered inside, holding it together for the rest of the family. He would bring his friends to the coffin, saying, "This is my grandson." I wanted to die.

Duane's family began to arrive on Friday, and the arrival of his oldest brother, Dwight, with whom he was always very close, allowed Duane to cry freely for the first time. All of Duane's brothers and sisters and their families came with his mother, Rose. Just a few short months before, on the Christmas before Andy died, Grandma Rose had given him one of his most prized possessions, a ladybug magnet that she had hanging on her refrigerator. That magnet now lay in his coffin near his head. He clutched in one hand a hand-painted pendant of St. George, given to him by his beloved Baba.

The funeral was Saturday morning with a viewing held first in church. I felt strangely peaceful with the casket open and Andy's body there in church. He belonged there where we had been married and he had been baptized. Father Rade Merick had baptized Andy: it had been his first baptism after being assigned there. And now Andrew was also to be his first child burial. At the funeral home, Father Merick was unable to speak upon first approaching us sitting at Andy's coffin. He knelt beside us. We took his hand and told him all about Andrew and his love for God, how he had tried to convert a Muslim, and a few of our favorite memories. We wanted everyone to know our son's spirit and that he was with God. This helped Father Merick a great deal and gave him something to add to the eulogy.

The church overflowed that day just as it had when we gathered there for joyous occasions. The people at Holy Resurrection did not look the other way in the face of our agony. They met it face-to-face.

At an Orthodox funeral the body is brought into the center of the church, and remains open until the end of the service. In our case, the priest performed the burial service for a child, and I must quote a few key elements that struck me then, and hold me upright now. [see Appendix]

The reading of the Holy Gospel during that service said, in part, "For I have come down from heaven not to do my will, but to do the will of Him who sent me. And this is the will of Him who sent me, that I shall lose none of all that He has given me, but raise them up at the last day." (John 6:38-39)

Later Father Merick recited this prayer: "By taking this child as a little bird to his heavenly nest, you have saved his soul from many snares and have united him with the souls of the righteous who are delighting in your Kingdom." I cried harder. I recalled how Andy had prayed to fly. His prayers had been answered. I hoped he was happy.

Father Merick's eulogy is preserved thanks to the kindness and forethought of a parishioner who taped Andy's funeral service, thinking that I might sometime want to listen to it again. Father Merick's sermon comes to my mind whenever I feel the loss of Andy "missing" growing up or getting married or having children of his own.

Father Merick began the sermon by reading the letter written by Father Ray, his "Reflections on Andrew", printed at the beginning of this book. Then Father Merick said, "We live in the world. Sometimes we are seduced by that world into thinking that its ways are the right ways. As Christians, we know that our whole being, our whole belief system is totally different than the ways of the world. All of us were stunned by this terrible tragedy. My first reaction was, God what could be worse? But you know, that's not a Christian reaction. If we listen to what we've said here today in this funeral service; listen to what those verses are telling us, it isn't the worst thing that could happen. The worst thing that could happen is not that someone dies. The worst thing that could happen is that when someone dies, their soul does not go to live with God."

"We are seduced by this world into thinking: this is it—that somehow everything that life has to offer, this life (on earth) offers. You think about all those things that Andrew missed by not growing up. But I don't think Andrew is missing anything. I know that he is not missing anything. If he were, we wouldn't be here today. The prayer that we read over the water at baptism is very important, and I read it now."

"For you are God, inexpressible, existing unto ages before ages, and ineffable. You descended upon earth and You took on the semblance of a servant and were made in the likeness of man. For because of the tender compassion of your mercy, O Master, you could not endure to see whole mankind oppressed by the devil, so you came and you saved us. So we confess your grace; we proclaim your glory. We do not conceal your mighty acts. You have delivered the generation of our mortal nature by your birth. You sanctified the Virgin's womb, and all creation magnifies you."

"And later in that same prayer," said Father Merick, "Therefore, O Lord, manifest yourself in this water and grant he who is baptized within it be transformed that he may put away from him the old man which was struck with the lust of the flesh and that he may be clothed with honor with the new man and renewed after the image of Him who created him that he.....after the pattern of your death and baptism, he may in like manner be a partaker in your resurrection. May he preserve the gift of your Holy Spirit and increase the measure of grace permitted unto him that he may receive the prize of his life calling and be numbered with the firstborn whose names are written in heaven. And you are God and Glory, Jesus Christ."

Father Merick continued, "I remember saying that prayer at Andy's baptism. I remember, you know, how in the Orthodox Church after a child has been baptized you put on their new baptismal garment to remind us that all of us who are baptized in Christ have put on Christ, and we wear Him now as a garment and that we are called to keep that garment pure and spotless until the day that we are called once again to appear before Christ so that we can appear in that garment. Appearing in that garment, He knows that we belong to Him, that we have a place in His heart. When we are baptized, we are baptized in Christ's name. We are baptized as preparation for this day. In baptism, you receive Christ, you receive the resurrection. You know that for most of us, we are struggling to keep that baptismal garment clean, that it might be suitable to wear in God's presence.

"Andrew has been saved from that fear. He doesn't have to worry about keeping his garment clean. It is spotless. We know that he is with God in His kingdom. That baptismal garment that he is wearing today is the garment of all clergy and all those who serve the church: the altar boy's robe; the deacon's robe, and the priest's robe. It's altogether appropriate that he is wearing that robe today."

"In the past few days, I've been talking with Sandy and Duane and to other members of the family, and what Father Ray says here is very true. They were telling me about the fact that they lost a babysitter, a Muslim one, because Andy was preaching to her son about Christ. Finally, the mother just could not have that anymore. How many of us take our baptism so seriously that we become missionaries? Yet a five-year-old child was able to. How many of us are willing to say Jesus Christ died for your sins?

"As we are here today, we think about last Sunday as he was going to serve. We know that he got there. He went to serve at an altar that was made by people, an altar that was made of metal and wood and stone, which is the shadow of the real altar which is in the Kingdom of Heaven. Andy got there, and he is serving at that altar. He is doing what he always wanted to do and what he loves to do. We can't weep for him; we can't if we know Christ.

"We weep for ourselves. We are going to miss him. I'm certain that as Andy looks on us, he says 'Why are you so sad? Isn't this what you told me it was all about in the first place? You told me that this was it, and now I see it.' So do not be too sad. I'm sure he stands before God's altar praying with us, and above all, praying for us. We ask that he continues to keep all of us in his prayers until that last day each one of us is reunited with him.

"May God give us the faith and strength to know His love, feel it, and trust Him with all of our being. So that we too may be able to share in the blessedness of the kingdom that He has prepared for us," he concluded. Father Merick had created a message of lasting significance for me, particularly in the last section about not being "too sad." These were words that I would hear from another, at least three more times.

After the homily, people approached the casket to venerate the Cross and kiss Andy for the last time while the priest read, "Suffer the little children to come unto me, for such is the Kingdom of

Heaven." I asked that Andy's cross be taken from around his neck. I needed it now much more than he did. I put it on, and have never, and will never take it off again. One of my sisters could not bear the thought of Andy being buried without a cross around his neck. She removed hers, and put it into the casket with him. Duane and I were the last to kiss Andy good-bye. I do not know how we did it. Even more difficult was seeing them close the casket right in front of our eyes. Blindness has always been a fear of mine. After seeing that sight, I wondered how I could go on seeing.

Andrew's godfather, his uncle, and his teenage cousins carried his casket to the hearse, and we drove through the cold to the cemetery. After a few short prayers, we placed flowers on the coffin. I sank to my knees clutching the casket. I was lifted away and put back into the limousine. My parents had arranged a catered lunch. As we began the procession back to the reception area, there was a single moment of comic relief. One of those attending the funeral passed the limousine in his hurry to get down the hill to lunch. At first, we all looked disgusted and could not believe that this person had passed us. No one said anything. Then I sighed and said, "Guess he was really hungry." We all started laughing. The limousine driver must have thought that we had lost our minds.

The luncheon provided an opportunity for us to visit with Duane's family and others. I spoke to Father Merick, telling him how much the service meant to us and how his words had helped not only us but also all those there present. He told us that it was our faith that had carried him through the difficult funeral and that we were "real Christians." I wondered at the time what he meant by that phrase. It would be only later that we encountered people who asked us how we could continue going to church after Andrew's death; how could we believe in a God that cared so little for us that he let our child die. One person even said, "You are good people. You go to church. You love your children. You work hard. How could God punish you like this?"

We had vague, occasional thoughts of being punished, in part because it is a predictable reaction to tragedy. A large part of grieving consists of our attempts to make sense of what has happened and it is only natural in the countless instances when we try to lay the blame for events that our anger and frustration ends up being turned upon ourselves. If we can blame someone or something, then our suffering can be made to make sense—and that process of finding the culprit is as ruthless and unsparing as it is automatic. Then came the saving reminder: God's justice is not of this earth. Here is free choice, and events that God chooses not to control. It is not at all in-accurate to say that we live in a world that have created, collectively and over the span of sin-drenched millenia. It is in such a world—a world of our own making—that our son died and it is a world in which his death has its meaning.

Arriving home after the funeral, everyone was exhausted. The garage had been filled with flowers brought from the funeral home, and the combined smell of them made me ill. I never wanted to see another flower as long as I lived. Some might think that the worst was behind us now that the funeral was over. But once we were home, we were left to face the terrible realization that our own worst nightmare had now become the rest of our life.

8

The Aftermath: How Do We Survive?

Dead silence prevailed after the funeral. With no arrangements to make, no one to take to the airport, no schedules to maintain, there was only silence, a silence larger and deeper than any I had ever encountered. Our son's presence, which used to shake the whole household, now became confined to a spot on the dining room table where his picture stood beside a vigil candle.

Each day was a struggle to survive. The most horrible part of the day was waking to discover the nightmare was still with us. Each day we faced the prospect of having to live one more day without our son. It was as though we were serving a life sentence in hell on earth. After about a week of this agony, we learned to begin praying while still semi-conscious. As I felt myself lifting from the blessing of sleep, I would begin to pray, asking God to be with me, help me, and strengthen me. I would then choose a happy memory of Andy to accompany me into wakefulness. This did not stop the tears, pain or nausea of waking up to a world without Andy, but it maintained my sanity.

The days were painfully alike; the horror of waking up, followed by going through the physical motions of dressing and taking meals. No one had much of an appetite. My mother would make a plate of toast and beg people to just have a few bites. Duane's broken shoulder blade made it impossible for him to even dress himself, so my father helped him shower and dress each day. Taking care of a nine month-old baby also was nearly impossible with our physical and emotional injuries. My parents loved and nurtured Ariana for us. In those first days after the funeral, it was difficult for us to feel anything for her or each other. We felt guilty that we were alive.

Through our shock broke the love of family and strangers alike. A day or two after the funeral, my Baba came running to the house with the portion of the money she had saved for Andrew as his inheritance. I could see that she was badly shaken. She would not rest until she had given us his money. She came dressed in a homemade black dress, but had forgotten to wear a slip under it. I could see a portion of her bra, a detail she would never have neglected had she not been so distraught. My Baba could be a harsh woman, coarsened by the weight of her hard life. She often offended people knowingly and unknowingly. But whatever pain she had caused, her saving grace was a spark of pure love that dwelt deep within her which, in this instance, was brought out by a devastating tragedy. I could not be glad for the money, but my heart will never be able to repay the love behind that gesture. I felt great compassion for her as we sat at the kitchen table, holding the sight of her in that black dress in my heart.

Several times Andrew's cross had fallen from my neck. His small chain was not big enough for me, so we ventured out to a jewelry store owned by Orthodox Christians who are friends of my parents. We stumbled into the store blindly. The manager asked us how we were.

He obviously did not know of our tragedy. No one answered him. "What's going on?" he asked . This was the first of many times when we would have to tell someone our son had died. We felt ashamed. "Our son was killed in a car accident. We buried him last week. This is his cross," I said pointing to my neck. "I need a heavier chain for the cross so that I will never lose it." His face crumpled as if someone had punched him. He looked about quickly for my father who had waited outside the store. Then he took a heavy gold chain with a safety clasp from the glass case and handed it to me. "These are strong," he said. "Take it."

I put Andrew's cross on the chain and clamped it securely around my neck. I took my checkbook out to pay the $250 marked on the price tag. "Will you take my out-of-state check?" I inquired. Tears welled in his eyes, "Take it," he said grasping my hands, "just take it." I thanked him and marveled that I not only had my son's cross around my neck, but also another gift given out of love from a man who was a stranger to me.

Relatives and friends from near and far came to visit and show support to us during those first forty days of mourning, and miracles began to happen right under our noses. Love and concern for us and our family overpowered family feuds, unresolved conflicts with friends, and deep-seated resentments toward each other. Thus began an unanticipated healing process within our own family, our extended families and church families.

We were brought great comfort on one occasion when Ariana's godparents, Joy and Duane, visited us at my parent's home in West Virginia. Joy shared with us a dream about Andrew. The dream was unusual, first because Joy seldom dreamed. She frequently awoke at night due to the pain in her back caused by fibromialgia, an arthritic condition. She rarely slept deeply enough to dream. Joy told us that she heard this dream but saw no images. It began when she heard the sound of a playground filled with children laughing, running, and playing. She heard a little boy say, "Hey, Andrew, here are your two brothers." In Andrew's characteristic way, he replied, "I already know that." The other boy replied, "Come on, let's go see Jesus!"

The days passed slowly as we recovered at my parent's home. We walked through the motions of living but felt little except the crush of our grief. Shortly after the funeral, Duane stopped talking completely. Each day we would visit Andy's unmarked grave. How I hated it there! I even hated Duane for taking any consolation in being there. Every time we visited the grave, I enacted the same ritual. I would approach the grave in anger and fear, sobbing. We would say the Lord's Prayer and then pray for Andy's soul. I would drop to the ground unable to believe what had happened. Duane would kneel lost in thought. Then I would storm away screaming, "He is NOT here!" leaving Duane torn between his dead child and angry wife.

When Duane stopped talking, I became even more angry. Days had passed and he had uttered only "yes" or "no" answers to questions. Then one day when we were visiting the grave, I swore against Duane with every oath I could remember. I was sick of his silence. I needed him to comfort me, but he could not speak. I realized we needed grief counseling if we were not going to let the devil, or ourselves, tear our family apart. We had to talk.

The realization that we needed counseling brought me back to the thought of our normal routines and the necessity of resuming them. We began planning to go back to Maryland, a task filled with fear and deep agony. We would be returning without Andrew to the places that he knew and loved. We would be leaving his physical remains high atop a hill in a cemetery. But we did not return alone. My parents accompanied us every painful step of the way.

The horror of walking back into our apartment without Andrew was compounded by someone who had taken down some of Andy's pictures and put many of his belongings out of sight. Even his drinking glasses had been removed from the kitchen cabinet. I went wild with anger and began searching for all his things and putting them back where they had been. He was dead, but I was not going to make him vanish. I will speak his name and recount his memory until the day I die. I do not believe in covering up the existence of a human being who has passed into God's world for the sake of sparing someone pain. What pain is greater than that of death or of nonexistence? For as long as I love my son, he is not dead. He lives in me, and I in him.

A huge box of cards and letters waited for us in Maryland. So many cards and letters had been written that it took us days to open them all. One, in particular, I will never forget. It was a short note written in a shaky handwriting, that I imagined to be that of an older person, saying she was a stranger but had read the newspaper account of the accident and grieved for us because nothing could be more horrible. She enclosed five dollars saying she would like to help us and maybe this could pay for a phone call home. It was love like this that gave us the courage to live.

Other strangers brought us blessings as well. A local TV newsperson called one afternoon. He had been filming a report at the accident scene and noticed many brightly colored papers littering the scene. Knowing that these must have belonged to the little boy who died there, he saved them for us. Our employers and coworkers also bolstered us. Each of our employers told us to take as much time off as we needed. People at each of our offices lined up to donate their vacation days to us so that we would not need to take any time off work without pay. Our church and our employers also took up collections for us to help pay funeral costs and to help us replace our car.

While I was on bereavement leave, my employers had arranged for counselors from the Employee Assistance Services to talk with my coworkers. Andy's death had devastated them. I had told so many "Andy stories" that even the people who had never met him felt as if they knew him personally. I changed positions every few years within my organization. Coworkers from previous assignments would call me and say, "Do you have any Andy stories? We were just talking about him and miss them!" The counselors were able to help them deal with their feelings of grief and confusion and give them some idea of how to support me when I returned.

I followed through with my intention to receive bereavement counseling in Maryland. In our initial meeting, I poured out my heart about my grief. I talked about God, saying we took comfort in knowing God and knowing that Andy was with Him. We felt that God had always been there for us. His love helped keep us alive. As I spoke these words, I noticed the counselor cross her legs and hold her notebook closer to her chest. That nearly imperceptible motion told me she did not believe. If she did not believe, I could develop no sense of trust with her. When the session was over, I knew I would never return to that office. We drifted for a week or two, not knowing what to do. Then one afternoon Father Ray called and asked if we were considering counseling and if I knew Carole, a psychologist who was attached to the same Employee Assistance Services that had already done so much to help my coworkers. I told him about the false start at our medical plan. He said, "Sandy, Carole is a member of our church. She was there at Andy's service at the funeral home. You may not remember her, but she says that you are able to receive counseling through work."

I called her immediately. Duane and I began to visit her office regularly. The counseling that we received there proved to be an irreplaceable anchor for us, particularly because it was administered not only with the deepest human compassion but also in a spirit of faith and love by another Orthodox Christian. The first few counseling sessions we scheduled for early afternoon. The appointments sped by quickly. We were amazed when we walked out of Carole's office into the dark of night. She initially spent up to three or more hours with us per session, allowing us to pour out our pain, anger, and frustration. She helped us channel those negative emotions into positive communications with each other so that our marriage could be kept alive. The statistics on divorce following the loss of a child propelled me into counseling in the first place.

Conservative estimates indicate that as many as seventy-five percent of the couples who lose children divorce. Some estimates are as high as ninety percent. I looked back over the handful of people we knew who had lost children. Only one couple had survived.

To aid our recovery, we also attended a Compassionate Friends meeting, the organization for people whose children have died that was recommended by our doctor. The bereaved parents sat in a circle. Each took a turn telling of their child's death. We were astonished and moved by the other tales of suffering. Hearing what the others had experienced was emotional shock therapy for us. Tragedy has a way of isolating the bereaved. Attending that first Compassionate Friends meeting gave us some perspective. We left the meeting consciously relieved that we were not alone in being singled out for such a fate. Yet it was disturbing to us that at the meetings a parent would tell a particularly gruesome story of their child's death, filled with minute details, sobbing and angry, and conclude by saying, "...and that was 15 years ago." For us, the thought of being stuck in this initial stage of grief for a decade or more was not appealing. It was also sobering to realize that many of the people in that room were taking prescription drugs as a means to fight depression. Some parents would sit chatting before the meeting began about their prescription types and dosage amounts. Other parents told stories of how they had survived. We went away from the meeting with an overwhelming impression of lives completely devastated. "We really don't belong here, Sandy," Duane told me after the first meeting. I agreed. There was something to be said, however, for being in a room where people understood what it was like to go through your son's clothes looking for something that still smelled like him. We would go back to those meetings again and again. Instead of dwelling on the details of our son's death, we found ourselves speaking a message of hope and survival.

Going back to work drained us of every ounce of energy; each day was a physical and emotional challenge. Flashbacks of the accident plagued me at work. During a meeting one afternoon, I began seeing the accident again, with Andrew crushed in the back seat and me standing outside helplessly. I looked upon his face, always pale, but now white in death. I felt a scream building inside me and wondered how I could go on when a heard his tiny voice inside me saying, "Not like that, Mom." He did not want me to remember him like that. He did not want me to remain at the scene of the accident for the rest of my life. This was the first time that Andy spoke to me. I marveled at his words and how this could be possible, and henceforth, every time I would begin to see the accident again, I would remember those words and move on. The flashbacks stopped.

My mom and dad stayed with us for a few weeks, helping us get through our initial period back at work. It was during that time that something odd happened. I was ironing in our bedroom and had walked away for a few minutes. Walking back into the bedroom, I smelled a strong, sweet odor, that quickened my heartbeat. I thought, "Andrew, are you here?" But I was afraid. I ran out of the bedroom asking, "Has anyone been spraying air freshener in here?" We did not use air freshener. I thought that someone might have bought some while we were away. I went into the bathroom to look for some. Then I went back into the bedroom and just sat there on the bed.

After the weeks of my parents helping us readjust, they departed. My mother left, in part, because she was concerned that I was not bonding with Ariana. I could tell by the way she kept putting Ariana in my arms all the time. I really did not want to be bothered. I just wanted to sit and stare. I had allowed myself to be absorbed by my pain to the exclusion of all interest in my daughter's needs, even the most rudimentary. I kissed her good night. My mother bathed, fed and loved her. We were thrown into deep shock when my parents left. Any little variation in our routine tore us apart. I could not sleep, although I continued working and caring for Ariana. My head hurt badly. Between the head injuries and the constant headache of no sleep, I felt only numbness.

Later that month in the dead of night, I lay alone on the couch. It was 3:30 in the morning. I watched the flickering light of Andy's memorial candle, wondering if I would ever sleep again. Too tired to even think, I simply stared. Suddenly, I was not alone in that room. My son's presence surrounded me. I could not see him, but I felt him there with me. My skin prickled. After a few moments, he spoke to me, not in words that could be heard by my ear, but in thoughts being exchanged. I recognized his voice in these thoughts, and he pleaded with me. "Mom, I want you to be happy." It was as though he were standing beside me wringing his hands. "Happy? Happy?" I shot back at him with all my unleashed anger and frustration. "You want me to be happy? I promised to survive, but you ask me the impossible. I can never be happy without you." My anger melted into sobbing, but my show of emotion did not daunt him. As he had been in this mortal life on earth, so even now Andrew remained confident. "If you won't be happy, then I will tickle you and make you happy." I was appalled and protested. "No, Andrew, No!" His presence spilled over me giggling. I laughed. He had his way one last time. Laughing helped me to let go of the blackness surrounding me. I drifted immediately into a deep, refreshing sleep from which I awoke with peace in my heart. My son was with me. He still loved me.

The pain of Andy's death remained with us, but it became bearable by hope, a hope that we all share because it is rooted in the resurrection of our Lord and Savior, Jesus Christ. I told Duane and my family of Andy's visit because I wanted to share the love, the hope, and the message that he wants us to be happy.

9

Our Transformation Begins

Returning to work was not the only difficulty that we faced during those first weeks back in Maryland. We also returned to St. Matthew's Church. Nowhere was Andrew closer to us, yet nowhere was his absence more pronounced and painfully apparent than in our small church. The Orthodox Church recognizes the health and necessity of going through the grieving process, and it aids in the psychological and emotional progression of that process by means of a series of commemorative services in which the deceased person is integrated into the continuing liturgical prayer life of the community. In the period after the funeral, memorial services are held at intervals of seven days, forty days, six months, one year, and each year after that on the anniversary of the death. One could say that, liturgically speaking, the Orthodox Church refuses to "let people die," in the sense that mortal death is never seen as being in any way final or absolute as far as the corporate prayer life of the worshipping community is concerned: the living continue to pray for those who have fallen asleep in the Lord.

Before Andrew died, I had thought that anniversaries were events to be celebrated. Anniversary now holds horrible new meaning for us. I had dreaded that forty-day service because it seemed like another funeral. I was burying my boy all over again. I completely lost my composure afterward, sobbing alone in the lobby of the church. Carole rushed to my side, took me in her arms and said, "This is not goodbye. You are not saying goodbye to him!" Her words calmed me immediately. I was reeling at the prospect of having to say goodbye to Andrew again and again because that is what people expected us to do. I was refusing to say goodbye to my child. I felt that to say goodbye to him would be to deny him. It was this understanding of the memorial service that I was struggling to overcome. My feelings had blinded me to the real message of the commemoration—that of greeting rather than departure, that we bear witness to the bond of prayer that still joins the living with those who have gone before us.

Over the next several weeks, we began to realize what was invoved in the purely physical ordeal of our grief, mustering all our reserves to get through a day. Duane had a particularly difficult time in the mornings because he dropped Ariana off at the sitter's house. Her brother was no longer there with her. On the very first day that Ariana arrived without Andrew, one of the other children asked Ariana where her brother was. It was a question that crushed Duane's heart. Each day, he would cry on the way to work, which was typically a commute of an hour or more.

It was during those first few weeks back at work that Duane was visited by an idea that he knew was not his own. Ever since the accident he had been troubled over the fact that he had not been with Andrew when he died. The accident had left him unconscious and of course the scene of the accident with Andrew trapped in the car was something that he knew only indirectly through what I was able to tell him. He felt that he did not have a chance to say goodbye and that he had failed Andrew at the moment of his death. It was during the short ride on the way to the sitter's house one morning, in the midst of one of those frequent intervals when the mind is not focused on anything in particular, that a thought presented itself to him with a remarkable fullness and clarity. He was assured that after the impact of the truck his own soul had touched Andy's.

A few days later, Duane shared that thought with me. He described how it occurred, commenting especially on the completely unanticipated manner in which it presented itself. When Duane told me about his conviction that he had touched Andrew's spirit, I responded, "You did, Duane. Your heart stopped beating when you hit the steering wheel. You looked dead. I screamed for you not to leave me to face this life alone, and grabbed your arm and began shaking you. After a minute, you sat straight up, looked me in the face, and fainted." He turned pale and, looking slowly away, dropped the subject.

My parents returned in April to help bolster our spirits. During their stay, we had a three-hour session with Carole after which we had some supper and then attended a Compassionate Friends meeting that lasted over two hours. Coming out of the meeting sobbing, I hit bottom. Some people at the meeting were talking enthusiastically about a British medium who contacted the spirits of those who had passed from this life. It was the last thing I wanted to hear and the thing I feared most. I lived in fear that I would see Andrew again and would then lose my mind because I would have to let him go, again. I even talked with Father Ray about this fear. He assured me that the Lord only gives us what we can handle.

Driving home from the meeting, I could not stop crying. After a while, Duane spoke to me quietly and with great purpose. "There is something about the accident that I haven't told you.

"Something happened to me. You know that I was knocked unconscious. I didn't regain full consciousness until I was in the ambulance. But I remember two things happening between the impact and my awakening in the ambulance. The chronological order of the two events is very clear in my mind. First, I remember being in the presence of a great white light, a radiance that filled up my entire field of vision. I remember looking up at it and being completely amazed, transfixed, and only able to contemplate its indescribably lustrous beauty: such a light as this I have never seen anywhere on this earth; it was a light of the most pearly white, incandescent radiance. I remember that I very much enjoyed looking at it. It was also quiet, a soft, cottony, comfortable silence that filled up all the space around me. And then I remember at some point in all of this, I heard you screaming; it started to break into the silence. It was as if you were not only distant but outside somewhere. Sandy, it was the strangest thing. The sound started very faint, but then it grew loud very quickly. Suddenly, it was as though I was crashing back into my body through my head, almost feeling the bulk of my body hit the car seat, and then you were screaming in my ear. I remember being alarmed and upset when I heard you screaming, opening my eyes briefly, and then falling back into oblivion. And second, I awoke there in the ambulance, freezing and immobile, staring up at the blurry, harsh light of the interior with all the commotion around me. I remember how comforting it was to hear Ariana's tiny cry somewhere near where I was lying."

We felt torn between two worlds. We were living in this one; but yet we yearned for the next. God was so real, but we could not touch Him, or Andy. How were we to live? Duane swore me to secrecy. When Duane told me of his experience it marked an important point in a much larger process in which we were beginning to realize that everything is ultimately about love—God's love for us and our love for each other. We began to feel gratitude in our hearts for Him, for our families, and for our church community. The trip home from the meeting that night was a moment that the two of us recall with a mixture of trembling and thankfulness. It was a moment in which we both came to a vivid awareness of God's power and love, and of His mercy even in the wake of our own searing tragedy. Indeed, "it is a fearful thing to fall into the hands of the living God." (Hebrews 10:31)

At the end of April we expressed this gratitude in a letter sent to the parishioners of St. Matthew's Church. It said:

"Words cannot express the depth of our gratitude to every one of you for the love, concern, and support extended to our family during this horrifying tragedy, the loss of our beloved son, Andrew. As soon as the community at St. Matthew's learned of Andrew's passing, everyone reached out to us with love, compassion, concern, and prayer. The community supported us and each other, cooked for us, and gathered funds to help ease the financial burden. We are eternally grateful.

"Andy's rapidly scheduled viewing on Tuesday at Fleck Funeral Home in Laurel was a testimony to the power of love and the presence of God in our lives. Much of that night is a blur to us, but the one memory that remains is the overwhelming sense of community, compassion, love and shared pain in the room that night. The death of one's child is a burden that cannot be borne alone, and thanks be to God that we have a multitude of people to share our grief and encourage our recovery. The funeral home showing in Laurel is one of the most comforting memories that we draw upon today. The funeral in Ohio was also comforting, and Andy belonged in that church in Steubenville where we were married and he was baptized, but St. Matthew's is our spiritual home, and we have been sustained by this special community. We are upheld by your prayers. The love that we feel flowing from you, like the hand of God himself, keeps us from falling into the depths of despair.

"While it is difficult to think that we are blessed, I believe that we are. God is everywhere in our lives pouring out His love. We thank God for each other, our daughter, our families, and for you, our brothers and sisters. Christ is with us; He is and always shall be.

Andy is also with us. To say that he is dead is to deny Christ and the Resurrection. Andy lives with Jesus, and we pray to be worthy to be lifted up to join him when we pass.

"We hesitate to ask for more from a community that has already given so much, but we do have a request. We will be writing a book about Andy and would appreciate it if each of you would write down your special memories of him and share them with us. As we move forward together, may the light of Andy's life show us the joy found in the pure love of the Lord. May we live lives well-pleasing to God and true to the memory of Andrew."

We survived by praying and feeling and expressing gratitude to God and our fellow human beings. Taking on works of charity eased our burden momentarily, but nothing erased our pain. Evenings took on an entirely new routine. Instead of watching television after the children were in bed, as we had when Andy lived, we began talking to each other. We were becoming increasingly tormented by the realization that we could not go on living as we had before Andy died; we felt caught between the two worlds and turned upside down. Everything that we thought was real, our earthly cares, had been supplanted by the knowledge of God's love, which had become the single most tangible fact in our lives. How, then, we were supposed to behave?

A transformation began. Before the accident, our lives had included God on our calendars when convenient. Now we desired a new life, one in which we sought Christ above all else. I learned that no matter how determined I was to seek Christ, I had actually to seek Him, not just desire seeking Him. I cannot control every situation. This lesson hit me one day after visiting the Greek section of Baltimore. There I had eaten at a restaurant with some friends from work, and I stopped to buy an icon. When I left my friend's van that afternoon, I took with me my leftover lunch and a magazine article I needed to read for work. I arrived home that evening to the horrible realization that I had left God behind. I had taken the two things that were most important to me, my food and my work, and had left God in the car.

Duane and I thought intensely over the next few months about a single question: how do we live in this world? We had stepped up works of charity, prayed together and alone more regularly, and listened to those in need, but it was not enough. Anything that we did left us feeling incomplete somehow.

During these next two months, we faced Pascha and St. George's Day without Andrew. Easter, needless to say, was very difficult. One of Andrew's aunts had bought him a large, wooden Easter basket painted in beautiful pastel colors. I looked at Andrew's name painted above a bunny rabbit that smiled stupidly at me. How could we ever fill this space? How much more energy could it take to endure this pain?

10

How Do We Live In The World?

We continued to think about how we should proceed with our lives. We could no longer look at God, life or even ourselves in the same terms. What had been our faith in God before the accident now became certainty that God, above all other things, is the supreme, living reality. We were now left with the search for the meaning of these changes in our lives. Driving home from work one day, I asked myself the question again: how do we live in this world? How do we best serve Christ? Suddenly an answer rang through my head. Duane was to become a priest.

This was not a novel idea. We had discussed his entering the priesthood occasionally over the years. But it seemed that whenever we had discussed this possibility we had no difficulty in arriving at reasons why we should not go to the seminary. The focus was invariably on money. We thought that we had too many financial obligations to go off to the seminary, such as our student loans and the other debts incurred while in graduate school. We had told ourselves that five years from now when the loans were paid off and the children were in school and would not need costly daycare, that then, and maybe only then, could we even think about going to the seminary.

Now everything had changed. When the answer came to me, I wondered how Duane would react. I waited that night until Ariana was asleep, and we began to talk. I started with what had by then become our nightly theme: how do we live in this world? Then I said to him, "We have said that in order to be able to live in this world we had to love God and his people above all else and to express that love in service? What better way is there to do that than by becoming a shepherd of His flock? You should become a priest!"

Instead of the shocked look that I had expected to see from my husband, he looked steadily at me. "I have reached the same conclusion myself, Sandy. When I turn over all that has happened to us, when I lay it all out in front of me and ask myself the question, what does it all mean, then I keep getting the same answer: Duane, you are to become a priest. There is nothing else left for you. But I'm not sure. I don't really know if I am worthy to be a priest."

For this I had an answer. "Jesus Christ is the only one to live without sin. Duane, no one is asking you to become Jesus Christ! It is God who makes you worthy to be a priest. If we love Him and His people, what greater service is there?"

Duane said that he needed to think this idea over carefully, which he did over the next few days. Then one evening he told me, "If a person is going to become a priest, then he has to experience a calling. I'm not really sure that I have." Fixing my gaze on him, I asked, "Look at everything that has happened to us. If that is not a calling, then I don't know what one is. Besides, who has to do the calling? We are called by the events of our lives and the example of our son. And if you feel you need something more concrete than that, then here, I'm calling you. Let God's calling come to you through me, your wife!"

Several days later, Duane told me he had reached a decision. He wanted, with all his heart, to go forward to do God's work. It was on that day that Duane told me of his secret desire to become a priest, a wish that he had kept within himself ever since his childhood. Now we were going to the seminary. This knowledge became a powerful secret between us. We kept this to ourselves until late May because we feared that people would question a decision like this coming so soon after Andrew's death.

In the meantime we busied ourselves with the daily marathon of trying to live through the day and its pain. We made our way with a powerful hope and purpose. Ariana's first birthday approached, a happy event marred by the tragedy of our son's death. For six years, I held beautiful birthday parties for our son. Now my daughter was turning one, and he was not with us. He would never have another birthday. I tried to muster some enthusiasm and ordered a Barney the Dinosaur cake for Ariana. I bought party items and vomited for a week.

In the following months, we continued to think through our decision to go to the seminary. I stayed home from work one day with a migraine headache and needed quiet and rest. I sat in a chair with a copy of the Orthodox Study Bible clutched to my chest and prayed for direction. I asked whether our decision to go to St. Vladimir's was the Lord's or ours alone. After sitting quietly for a time, I opened the Bible randomly to a passage from 2 Corinthians that read as follows:

> "Now I rejoice, not that you were made sorry, but that your sorrow led to repentance. For you were made sorry in a godly manner, that you might suffer loss from us in nothing."

> "For observe this very thing, that you have sorrowed in a godly manner: What diligence it produced in you, what clearing of yourselves, what indignation, what fear, what vehement desire, what zeal, what vindication! In all things you proved yourselves to be clear in this matter."

My eyes were then drawn to the closing verse of the chapter, "Therefore, I rejoice that I have confidence in you in everything." [2 Corinthians 7:9-16]

We had our answer and told Father Ray about our plans. We also told my parents. They were shocked and reminded us that in counseling we had been told not to make any major decisions for a year after Andy's death. But these were not normal circumstances. My parents, as always, promised to support us in whatever we decided to do. They approached us cautiously as did many people. Some looked at us with a mixture of horror and bewilderment when we revealed our decision to go to the seminary. Others talked with us as one would with the mentally disturbed. But we now had a new reality and a vision. We were determined to keep moving forward despite being overwhelmed time after time by our acute pain. Sometimes we would cry out in anger and frustration, causing the same reaction in little Ariana.

My first separation from Ariana was at the hospital after the accident when she remained in infant intensive care. Regretfully, I allowed my grief for Andrew to create a longer emotional separation from her. Ariana felt these things acutely. If she heard me crying, she would begin to scream, shrieking, as she did at the scene of the accident. Therefore, I had to learn to cry on the way home from work each night. Driving between the office, where I had to remain composed all day, and the sitter, where I picked up Ariana, I had about 15 minutes that I would use to cry, scream, and shout my anguish. During one particularly bad episode of screaming and crying, I just wanted to be dead so that the pain would stop. I could not stand another moment of this life without Andrew. I was interrupted in mid-scream by Andrew's voice speaking inside my heart. He sounded puzzled. "But Mom, I am with God."

"I don't care," I screamed back, "I want you here with me!"

So it came to pass that, just as Father Merick had said in his eulogy for Andrew, we cry not for the departed, but for ourselves. We had told Andrew what being with God was all about, and he is with Him. In my selfishness, I would deny my son living in the glory of God because I miss him so. God forgive me. The argument with Andrew calmed me and gave me something more to think about.

Suddenly it was summer. The beautiful flowers and renewal of life was wasted upon us that year. It seemed only to accentuate our pain by making the death we lived with each day also filled with flowers and budding trees. The sounds of children joyfully playing outside filled us with nausea, especially on the Fourth of July, one of Andy's favorite holidays. How he loved the fireworks, especially when we went with a group from St. Matthew's Church as had become our custom in the past few years. This Fourth of July we accepted no invitations. We locked the door of our apartment on Friday night and did not go out again for two days. We did not eat. We did not open our drapes. We could hear families outside playing with their children. They barbecued. It was agony to us. Our house was silent. Gone was the whooping and hollering of our little Ninja Turtle. Gone were the incessant questions and pleas. Our boy was gone. The silence in our home was interrupted by Ariana's occasional crying. We barely spoke all weekend. On Monday, I ventured out for some groceries and fell down the steps. I could not feel them beneath my feet. As I fell, I did not even feel myself hit the ground…

Work began again on Tuesday, and I began Grand Jury Duty that week. Every Tuesday from July through September, I was scheduled to serve on the Prince George's County Grand Jury. The judge had chosen me as the foreman. Some people who were concerned about me suggested that I ask to be dismissed from duty because of my son's death. I refused to use his death as an excuse for anything.

The grand jury reviews between twenty and thirty cases a day in order to decide whether there is sufficient evidence to issue indictments and bring the case to trial. Our particular jury heard cases of rape, attempted murder, assault with intent to kill or maim, child abuse, and child pornography. The evil that had been so abstract for me in the world suddenly began to have faces and victims. Hearing these cases sharpened my sense of what is truly evil. I then understood that evil is not a part of us unless we choose it. As Father Ray instructed me, mingled in our consciousness there are a number of voices: our own voice, the voice of God, and the voice of evil. I gradually learned to call evil by its name and ask it to depart.

One time in particular, I remember I had gone to the drug store. On the way home, I was crying in the car, as usual, and a thought occurred to me. "You were not good enough to be Andy's mother. That's why he was taken away from you." I panicked. Of course it was true. I was a wretch. I was wicked. I did not deserve such a son. I was not a good enough mother, or he would not be dead.

I screamed and sobbed my way home. I could not stop when I arrived. I emerged from the car sobbing. I ran to our bedroom where I cried until I had no more strength. In the quiet moments that followed that descent into hell, I understood that the devil, finding me in a weak moment, amplified doubts about myself and my responsibility for Andy's death and tried to separate me from God by making me believe that I was unworthy of love, unworthy of Andrew, and that God was punishing me. I knew in my heart that this was not true. Not only was it not true, the suggestion was purely evil. I cast it out by calling its name. I said aloud, "Satan, get thee behind me."

During jury duty I learned about the hell that violence against each other can play among families and through society. I saw the lies people believe to perpetuate these evil acts. People asked me how I was able even to stand this jury duty. I did not know. I just did. I had to learn. Soon I was to understand why.

11

Alive In Christ

The second week in July I was sleeping peacefully when suddenly my son stood before my eyes. He stood erect, stately. "Look at me," he spoke soothingly. He was beautiful. Light burst from him everywhere. He spread his arms out to me. Light burst from between his arms and sides, even from between his fingers. His face was wise, not smiling, but filled with knowledge and peace, love and strength. That look is indescribable. He was still a child, but did not have the same body. He was slightly taller and much more muscular. It looked as if he had been weightlifting, there was such strength in his shoulders.

Andy was dressed in a white and gold robe, similar to his altar boy's robe. This robe was larger and more flowing. He stood confidently, allowing me to take this all in. I was in awe, struck dumb by this sight. Is this really my child? I wondered.

"This is what I am now, Mother." I could not respond. I froze. I could not fill my eyes enough with the sight of him. Still staring, I watched Andrew draw his right hand around to his side, light slicing through the surrounding darkness. He reached into the darkness and pulled around to his chest a huge, unlighted taper, of the kind that is lighted and carried during the reading of the Gospel during the Divine Liturgy. "Everything will be OK," he said.

When Andrew pulled the candle to the center of his chest, the wick burst into a bright flame. Illuminated in the darkness behind him was my eighty-seven-year-old Baba, sitting behind Andrew on a wooden chair. She was not flowing with light like Andy. Dressed in her blue and green flowered dress, she was sitting with her hat and purse as if she was waiting to go on a journey. I sat straight up in bed in a cold sweat. "She is with me," Andy said, extending his arm protectively to her as though to say he would take care of her. And he departed.

I bolted up from bed. It was three a.m. I could not call anyone. Oh God, I thought, had she already died, or had Andy just shared a vision of things to come? Don't I get a chance to say goodbye, to tell her that I

am sorry for all the bad things that had happened between us, to ask
her to forgive me, to tell her that I forgive her, that I love her? I had to
wait until morning. I eventually went back to sleep, and jumped out of
bed in the morning. Dialing Baba's number, my heart was bursting in
my chest. After it rang several times, she answered sleepily. "Oh, Baba!"
I embraced her with my voice. "We miss you! How are you?"

"Never mind me," she said curtly. "How are you?"

"We miss you, and we love you," I told her. "I know we've had
problems in the past, but I want to tell you that none of that matters.
I love you. This baby loves you. My husband loves you, and we're all
thinking of you."

"I love you, too," she said, which were words she did not often
speak to me. "But just promise me one thing. Don't be broken down
about Andrew. It is a sin to cry so much. Don't disturb his peace."

"I won't be broken down, Baba. I told Andrew before we buried
him that I would have died for him a thousand times, but I was not
given that choice, so the only thing I could do now is to live for him,
the way he would have lived. No, Baba, I won't be broken down
about Andrew. You will see him before I do. Please tell him how
much I love him."

"I will," she promised, and we said our goodbyes.

I told my husband, Father Ray, and my parents and sisters to be
prepared for another death in the family. Coming so close on the
heels of Andrew's death, I knew it would be a horrible ordeal for the
entire family. Little did I know just how horrible.

We visited Baba at her home about a week later. She seemed
strangely at peace and moved with an air of soft resignation. After we
left, Duane and I both remarked on her demeanor, how she seemed to
be letting go of life and accepting that it was time to pass on, although
she had no real threats to her health. She shared a dream with us in
which her husband had come to her and sat at the foot of her bed. My
Jedo[1] told her that everything was going to be all right. She apparently
believed that it would be. He also told her she should be careful.

My mother arrived for a visit in Maryland a few days later on another mission of mercy. At church on Sunday, Father Ray inquired

---

1 Serbian for 'grandfather'.

about my grandmother, remembering what I had told him of my vision. My mom told him that Baba was fine. Whatever her health at the moment, Fr. Ray said he felt glad, thinking that whatever happened, at least I had made peace with my grandmother.

That Tuesday when I came home from jury duty, my mother and Ariana were not at home. Seeing that the car was not in the parking lot, I drove to the mall to surprise them. They were not there. I came home and, upon entering the door, I saw Ariana's car seat. It had been taken out of my mother's car and put beside the door. I knew instantly that my mother had taken Ariana to the sitter, removed her car seat and was now on her way to West Virginia. Something terrible had happened.

I walked straight to the phone and called my father. His voice was heavy. "Dad, what happened," I asked, my heart racing. He said nothing, and I waited.

"Your Baba is dead," he finally said.

I told him how sorry I was and asked what had happend.

"Is anyone there with you?" he asked.

"No," I replied, "But you don't have to worry about me. What can you tell me that is any worse than what I've been through?"

"Sandra," he said slowly. "Your Baba was killed."

"What do you mean killed," I asked, my voice getting louder.

"Baba was murdered."

It was three weeks after my vision, and another tragic ordeal began, not quite six months following Andrew's death. I began packing to go home.

The murderer entered Baba's house through the front door, punched her in the face, stabbed her twenty-seven times, slit her throat, and then beat her head in with her own cane. He fled out the back door taking her cane and the knife used to kill her. My father found her body the next morning when he went to check on her to see if she needed anything as he did everyday. He knew that one day he would find her taken by death, but not this way.

Baba was in the same funeral parlor as Andrew had been. She was in the same room, the casket up against the same wall, the sickening smell of flowers and death everywhere. We had to have a closed-casket funeral because her body was mutilated. For family members, there was a brief, open-casket viewing. Baba was nearly unrecognizable except for the beautiful dress she had made for herself to be buried in. Through the lace of the dress, I could see knife slashes on her arms where she had apparently tried to defend herself. Her head was so badly crushed that the embalming fluid was running out of it onto her pillow in the coffin. We had no tears left. The police quickly apprehended a suspect, a young man who had been one of my grandmother's neighbors. He had been out on bail for five days awaiting trial on charges of attempted murder, kidnapping, and robbery from a previous incident. This nineteen-year-old child, Scott Kenneth Howell, had mowed my grandmother's grass, along with another neighborhood boy. She would pay them, bring them into the house and feed them, and in the best old-world way, tell them what to do with their lives.

The night of the murder Scott Howell had attempted to break into another neighbor's garage, presumably to steal something, but he had been caught in the act, and the neighbor had struck him in the head, apparently making him very angry. He ran down the hill, borrowed a cigarette from a group of neighbors sitting on the porch, smoked it, panting heavily, and then went to my grandmother's home, taking my grandmother's life and nothing else in the house. From the scene of the murder, he went with the knife to a party, covered in blood. He had hidden the cane with which he had bludgeoned my Baba in the cemetery behind her house. His girlfriend hid the knife for him at her own house, in the wastebasket in her bedroom. My grandmother had made that knife herself. She could make all kinds of things and, in fact, she had been making a purse when she was murdered.

We know these details from witness testimony and from Scott Howell's own statements. He confessed to the murder a few days before he was scheduled to go on trial. News of the brutal murder had been broadcast all over the tri-state area of Ohio, West Virginia, and Pennsylvania. It was even covered by some national networks and USA Today. We became the objects of curiosity. My mother would not even buy her groceries in town; she did not want to sign a check lest someone recognize the name upon it.

We buried Baba in the cemetery behind her home next to her husband, a place she had longed to be since his death thirteen years earlier. Our family was devastated once again. For us, evil now had a face. We watched it on the evening news. Scott Howell appeared on television with dark, staring, soulless eyes, a pale child who barely looked like he was even fourteen years old. In our grief we despairingly wondered what could be so wrong in his life that he would do such a thing? Abandoned alongside a highway at the age of eight, Scott Howell was adopted by a professional family in Weirton who tried to save him. I wanted to see his head bashed in as did the rest of my family.

My father had to testify in open court in preliminary and bail hearings, which the local television and press covered. The killer's picture with that evil hollow look stared at us from the front pages of the newspapers, and all the world read our father's choked testimony of how he found his mother dead. Yet, in the midst of all this pain, the vision of Andrew and Baba together gave us all hope and a chance to heal. My parents, sisters, and other relatives asked me to describe the vision again and again. We believed Andy's words: "She is with me." We prayed that God would at last grant her the rest and the serenity that she did not have on this earth. We sometimes laughed, envisioning Andy and Baba continuing their bickering together in Heaven.

August was a traumatic month in more ways than one. After Baba's funeral on 6 August, we had to begin preparing for Andrew's six-month memorial service, which was held about two weeks later. I prepared myself by trying to get up the courage to cancel the memorial service. I did not want to go through anything else.

In searching for ways to help us struggle through yet another trauma, Carole suggested that it might be good for Father Ray to add something to the traditional memorial service by saying something about Andrew and how he is remembered. The memorial service comes at the end of the regular liturgy at which time the priest says the prayers for the departed and blesses the kolivo, a mixture of boiled wheat and honey, symbolizing life everlasting, in which a candle burns. We sobbed through most of church in anticipation of the service, and my husband had to hold me upright through the memorial service itself. The choir sang the beautiful "Memory Eternal," reminding us that when all passes away, Andrew will eternally be in God's memory. But I was angry. I did not want a memory. I wanted my son. Father Ray said some words about how Andy is remembered in our community and in churches around the country. I thought about how some people in our congregation, and other Orthodox Christians, people we had never met, were beginning to call him a saint—Andrew, the little altar boy from Columbia. Father Ray went on talking about Andrew and pointed out that his own children still speak of Andy in the present tense. He related a conversation with his son after Andy's death in which Craig said, "Andy is an altar boy." "Yes," Father Ray said. "He is serving at the Lord's table."

By the end of August, we really needed to get away somewhere, anywhere. My parents would not budge, but my sisters, Duane, and I went to a ski lodge in the woods of central Pennsylvania, just for some quiet time. We talked, ate, prayed, and walked in the woods trying to make some sense of our lives. On the return trip from this retreat Duane and I stopped at the Antiochian Orthodox Village in Ligonier, Pennsylvania, in order to see an iconographer of whom we had heard many good things. When we arrived we were told that Philip Zimmerman was not expected in that day, and after a brief tour of the facility, we turned to leave. On our way across the parking lot a car pulled up and out stepped the man we sought. As we were introduced, Philip explained that it had not been his intention to come there that day, but that he decided to drop by anyway and take care of some things. Duane and I had felt compelled to make this visit and now it seemed as though our meeting was destined to take place. We had been drawn to him. We knew that we had to tell him our story. We had first heard of Philip Zimmerman through Margo and David Sinkevitch, a St. Matthew's couple who had visited Ligonier earlier that year. Margo told us how much the story of Andrew's life and death had meant to her father, a priest in Michigan. He devoted a homily to Andrew, and they hung Andrew's picture next to the memorial candles. He is remembered every week in that community and in many other parishes. Margo and David told us that Andrew reminded them of another child saint, Artemius of Verkola.

St. Artemius was born in Verkola in 1532 and lived a pious life. When he was twelve, he died during a thunderstorm as he worked alongside his father in the fields. The villagers of Verkola believed that the clap of thunder over the boy's head before his death had been a judgement against him by God and would not give him a funeral or bury his body. It remained above ground, without a coffin, covered only by branches and birch bark. Thus his body was found thirty-two years later, incorrupt with light shining above it. His relics produced healings among believers, and the church of St. Nicholas began to commemorate the Righteous Child Artemius. In 1918, after multiple healings and other miraculous works, the relics of St. Artemius were destroyed. One *synaxarion*[2] stated, "In the summer of 1918, the Soviets began their systematic mockery and destruction of holy things, in particular the holy relics of Saints, and the relics of St. Artemius had the honor of enduring the first martyrdom at the hands of these God-haters. His relics were chopped to pieces and thrown into a well. And so the seed of one pious and holy childhood became a fruit of blessing and spiritual power for a whole multitude of Christians for centuries, and even the martyrdom of his holy relics cannot obliterate the memory of the Saint from their hearts, nor his intercessory power before the throne of God."

Philip knew nothing about St. Artemius before being visited by the child saint in a series of dream visions. St. Artemius instructed him about the painting and showed him flowers to include in it. Even after painting the child, Philip did not know who he was, but through a series of "coincidences" discovered that he had been visited by St. Artemius. By trusting us enough to reveal his own personal experience of these visions to us, Philip helped to lessen my fear of having seen Andrew in the way that I did. I believe that if I had not had those conversations with Philip, I might never have had the courage to put Andrew's life on paper. It was just too frightening to me. But Philip had heard of Andrew, and felt that he already knew us. Our visit there marked the third time that someone had told him Andrew's story. The first was Margo and David Sinkevitch, of our parish, but the second puzzled me. They were a Greek Orthodox couple from Maryland, whom we did not know. Philip reassured me again. He said, "Everyone has heard about the little altar boy in Columbia. His story is spreading throughout the Orthodox community." We talked with Philip for over three hours. We told him that we felt the Holy Spirit had led us to him, and in his charming way, he responded, "Well, I should hope so! God forbid it should be otherwise!"

As we departed, Philip gave us a powerful icon he had painted of Jesus with the children. He had modeled one of the children's faces after a sixteen year-old child who had died in a car accident. When I

2 A compendium of the lives of the saints arranged calendrically with each saint or group of saints being listed on the day when they are commemorated.

tried to buy additional icons for my mother and Ariana, he just pressed them into my hand, taking no money, and bade us farewell. We agreed to stay in touch, and when we arrived back at my parent's house, we were very excited and told them all about Philip. I also called Father Ray immediately to tell him. He listened intently to everything I had to say, and then said he had something to tell me.

"Sandy," he said. "You know that our Sunday School director is getting ready for the new church school year to begin. She has found something that could be very upsetting, and is beside herself. I've told her that you and Duane are very spiritual people, and this only confirms what you already know."

"What is it, Father?" I asked, my stomach churning.

"Sandy, it is Andrew's Sunday School notebook. There are only two pages. The first is the story of St. Stephen."

"Yes, " I remember it. " I said.

"The second page is a drawing Andrew made of a truck hitting a car, and a child lying alongside the road." Father Ray then asked me if indeed Andrew had been lying alongside the road. His understanding was that Andrew was not thrown from the car but had died in the back seat. I explained to him that after the paramedics took Andrew from the car, they put him on a stretcher, laid it alongside the road, and tried to revive him.

The next Sunday I received the notebook. My hands trembled. Andy had colored the notebook with remarkable colors, the significance of which I did not immediately undestand. As usual, Andrew had written his name inside it. It reminded me that Miss Codd, his kindergarten teacher, had been mystified that Andrew had to write his name on everything, even places it did not belong, like on his bunk bed. She had said, "This isn't behavior typical of a six year-old." And now I knew that Andy, in his own beautiful way, was trying to leave as much of himself behind for us as he possibly could.

I looked at the story of St. Stephen, the first martyr. I turned the page, and there beneath a brightly colored sun, my boy drew the scene of the accident and himself lying alongside the road in the exact spot the stretcher had been located with two stones sailing in the air toward him. He had combined the elements of his own death with that of St. Stephen, who was stoned to death for his love of the Lord. My intuition that Andrew had known he would die was confirmed.

Just as the church school year had begun, so too, the regular school year was beginning. We watched going back-to-school activity all around us. We were sick. Andy would have been entering the first grade, a full day at school. He would have finally gotten to eat in the cafeteria and could have joined the soccer team. He needed no lessons now. Despite our faith, our pain was raw. One morning that September, we had car trouble. Duane took our car to the garage, which was near our home and the elementary school. It began raining as he walked home from the garage. As he approached the school, he began to move among the throngs of children and then he saw a familiar face. It was a little girl, a playmate of Andy's. She approached Duane and said, "Didn't you used to have a little boy named Andy?"

"Yes, I did," Duane said.

"I remember him," she continued. "I used to play with him."

"Yes," I remember you, too." Duane responded, and she ran off to be with her friends.

Duane crossed over the small footbridge behind the school. When he was alone, he began crying. Sobbing deeply, his pain overwhelmed him. He reeled once again with the familiar wish to be dead. As he moved across the open field in the pouring rain, he screamed for his son, "Andrew, Andrew!"

Only a parent who has buried a child can imagine the sound of that scream. He walked to the top of a hill, closed his eyes, sank down to the ground in the downpour, crushed by what he was feeling. It was precisely at that moment that there came a tremendous rushing sound, so sudden that it frightened him half out of his wits. It was in this shocked state that he turned and saw an entire flock of Canadian geese taking flight. Duane stood there, his mouth fully open and his eyes still bulging out in shock as they took off right in front of his face. His eyes followed the flock as it flew up over the school, circled around it, and then headed north in the direction that the accident had happened. The whole episode had a tremendous purging effect on Duane. It completely emptied him out, both psychically and emotionally, and left him in a calm, almost transfigured state of mind. He made his way back to our apartment, filled with an awareness of Andrew's presence, even in death. Duane had always associated Canadian geese with Andy. They used to watch large flocks of them gather together in the fields near my parent's house. It was after the funeral that he told me of the almost totemic identification with them that he had come to feel—that they were birds, their "honkers." Whenever Duane sees these geese, he still thinks of Andy.

The very next month, Duane had another experience. He was driving to work crying and again in his anguish he wished that he were dead. Through his tears of misery, he heard Andy's voice inside him saying, "Daddy, don't be sad. I am so happy." This communication from his son stopped his grief cold. He spent the rest of the day giving thanks to God for what had happened.

We passed through the rest of the autumn in stops and starts, with every holiday and special event a painful experience in that first full year after Andrew's death. In November, we had cause to be uplifted when, at our church, Nick Theodorakis was ordained a sub-deacon and Duane was tonsured a reader by our bishop, Metropolitan Theodosius. It was a happy time to be making our first step toward the service of our Lord, but as with any grieving parent, there is never any one single emotion. Every second of joy is tinged with pain, pain that we could not share that moment with our son, or so I thought. That night I saw Andrew again, for what I believe will be the last time until the day that, by God's grace, I am lifted up to join him for all eternity. In this vision, we exchanged no words. Andrew appeared to me as I was taking communion. He hovered above the ground close at my right shoulder as I received the body and blood of our Lord and Savior Jesus Christ.

Despite all the times that I have taken communion, since I was six weeks old, I had not fully understood what I understand now. This cloud of witnesses, the holy Orthodox faithful, is real. They stand with us at the cup united in Christ. I felt the peace and energy to continue. I told Duane of the vision immediately, but in all the flurry of activity surrounding that event, I had not told Joy. I called her on Monday night to tell her about seeing Andrew again. I hung up the phone and went back to my ironing. A few minutes later the phone rang. It was Joy, who was breathless. "Sandy, you will not believe what just happened! After we talked, I took out the pictures I got developed from the ordination that I hadn't had a chance to look at yet. I took over 100 pictures, and there is only one picture with anything wrong with it. It is a picture of you taking communion, and above your right shoulder is a smudge of light." Father Ray had always told us that there were no coincidences; that there is only God.

We moved on through the month of November. Despite the hope with which we lived, Thanksgiving was hell. Were we supposed to be thankful that Andrew was dead? I wanted Andrew to be with me, so I wrote him a letter.

November 21, 1994

Dear Andrew,

Mommy is making a list of everything to pack for Thanksgiving to take to Kuma[3] Joy's house, and I can't leave you out. I put your name on the list, but all I can pack for you is that love for you that I carry with me everywhere and always. I don't know how it is possible to feel so empty without you but so full of love at the same time.

I often tell people that for Daddy and me, the unseen is sometimes more real that what we can see, touch, and taste. I wish those moments were longer and that we could be in constant communion with you and our loving God. Please help us get there, son. Hold us up, for we fall often. Guide and pray for us. Please forgive us our sins and transgressions that we committed against you and others. Love us, Andy, especially Daddy. He needs you to help him express, feel and work through his grief. He has many dark moments in his soul that he cannot bring himself to share with me. I become angry because I fear I will drown in my own grief while he keeps his hidden inside.

We need your help at Thanksgiving, Andy, for it is hard for us to give true thanks. We feel we have been cheated, singled out for a life sentence of punishment that is indescribable. Most days are good. We love the possibilities that lie before us in our new life. But other days, especially the holidays, drain us of our resolve, leaving us weak and numb, dazed for the loss of you.

Yesterday's sermon was about cultivating things that we can take with us beyond death, where the rust and the moth do not consume. Love is the only thing that we can take with us, Andy. Mommy knows that. Please let me feel the love that you have taken with you for me, Daddy and Ariana. Please let me know that you can feel our love as well.

3 Serbian for 'godmother.'

How can I still be a mother to you Andy? How shall I proceed with the book? I pray you to guide me with the Father, Son, and Holy Spirit.

Mommy loves you, always in Christ

Once we got through Thanksgiving, we faced the horrifying prospect of Christmas without Andrew. December was a nightmare: the flurry of Christmas shoppers, decorations, and pain, such pain that I could not even take out the Christmas ornaments and put up a tree for my little Ariana. Instead, I bought a few special ornaments of the Virgin Mary, Jesus, and some angels and placed them around the house. Each day of this season dragged on like a physical torture. We were exhausted with the daily struggle of trying to survive it.

One morning as I stood in front of the mirror getting ready for work, sick with grief, I was thinking, "I can't buy him Christmas presents. He can't come with us to choose a tree and decorate it. He won't be there to open presents with us." Suddenly, I realized that none of those activities I had just listed to myself in anguish had anything to do with the birth of the Son of God, Jesus Christ. If it were not for the birth of Christ and His saving death and resurrection, we would not have life everlasting! This is the reason for a joyful season. And this is the reason we must live and truly celebrate the holiday.

For Christmas, I asked all our family to take the money they would have spent on Andrew and give it to charity, or find a needy family, or buy a needy child or adult something special. I also asked them to write Christmas cards to Andy, telling him how they were helping people in his and Christ's name. I wanted to read the cards aloud after we opened our presents on Christmas morning. I wanted Andy to be part of our celebration. The thought of this ceremony after the package opening was too great for some members of the family who felt it was better to keep a lid on the grief, especially around the young children. This was particularly true of my mother who told me that she could not even bring herself to write his name on a card. She agonized over it night after night; weighing her inability to write a card to Andy against her mother's instinct of trying to do everything she could for her own daughter who needed her.

In the hectic days of pre-Christmas shopping, my mother was in a card store writing a check for her purchase when something caught her eye. It was a tiny crystal clown holding red and green balloons.

When she saw the clown, she had the irresistible urge to buy it. She said she could almost hear it calling to her, "Buy me! Buy me!" But she could not understand why she should buy a crystal clown. She had been looking for something to buy for me from Andrew. She knew that I did not particularly like crystal. What she did not know at the time was that Andy loved it. He was always begging me to buy it. She left the store without the clown. After shopping in several other stores, she was drawn back to it. Examining the crystal clown, she wondered why on earth she should buy this thing, and then saying, "All right, already!", she bought it. That night she took pen and paper and went into the guest bedroom. There hung Andy's picture framed with his artwork, a Christmas present to our family that Duane and I had given several years before Andy's death. Mom intended to write some memories of Andy as her gift for me. She began:

Sandy,

Your request to do something this Chistmas in Andy's name for the poor needy has been granted. I won't list those things right now, instead I'd like to do "something special" *for* Andy. I want to just remember a few of his favorite things: The Land Before Time, Ninja Turtles...he loved his collections, rocks, (plastic) bugs, two seashells from the beach, "Baba, is this a collection?"

He loved talking you into things and then taking over, he loved stylish clothes, all of the things he loved could fill a book, but one of his most favorite things was his "funny stuff."

As I remember a few of Andy's favorite things, I now, in his memory, recall his most favorite thing, the spirit of fun and laughter, given to him by his beloved clown, his mother. The most famous form of flattery is imitation, "Am I your funny boy, Mom?" He always tried to emulate his favorite clown. He copied your style and inherited your intellect, "I already know that."

He admired you, "You look beautiful, Mom." He adored you and loved your sense of humor, so for Andy, and in his memory I give you a small crystal clown.

At that point my mother stopped writing. She had no idea why she was giving me a crystal clown besides what she had already written about fun and humor. She stared at Andy's picture in anguish mixed with curiosity. She said to herself, "OK already, why do I have this clown?" She doesn't know how long she sat there staring at his picture. Then, she felt Andy's presence. He told her that she had to help his mother. He told her about the clown. My mother copied what he said in her notebook.

The crystal as the sunbeams dance off it, remind us although we can't hold a sunbeam or a spirit, they both surround us constantly. The clown is to remind us how happy Andy was and is and to remind us all to be happy and joyful in Christ.

The crystal and the clown together make us aware that as long as we keep that spirit of love and laughter, that is Andy alive, and he will always be with us. The red and green balloons symbolize the spirit of Christmas and the celebration of the birth of our Lord, without whose birth, there would be no, resurrection. God be with you. I love you.

Nothing like this had ever happened to my mother. She told me on Christmas day, but asked that I not tell everyone right away. She was afraid that people would think she was crazy.

Joy and Duane also experienced Andrew's presence in a very special way that first Christmas. Joy did not want to celebrate the holiday that year. Without having us in Maryland for Christmas and knowing that Andrew was gone, she became very depressed. She had just hung up the phone from talking with me and wondered how any of us could go on when she looked at her icon shelf and saw a familiar little green bird sitting next to the icon of Christ.

"Where did that come from?" she asked her husband.

"I found it wedged between the couch and the recliner," he answered.

Joy told him that bird had belonged to Andrew. He had kept it in a little cardboard box with a blanket, and had lost it at their house. She and Andy had searched everywhere for that bird. It was nowhere to be found. That day, when she most needed it, it appeared among the saints where Andrew now dwells.

My mother and I soon learned that every single member of our family had a vision of Andrew in which he was happy, at peace, and told them that everything would be all right. Parishioners at St. Matthew's also began to come forward saying that they had felt Andrew's presence in a particularly difficult situation, and he had helped them. One parishioner did not know Andrew personally when he died. She had just begun coming to church at St. Matthew's and had seen him serve. She later told us that Andrew came to her in one of her darkest hours as she sat, broken and weeping, at the bedside of a loved one at the hospital who had bone cancer and was writhing in pain. She said that suddenly she felt an overwhelming peace, and she knew that Andrew was in the room. It helped her to know that everything would be fine, whatever the outcome of the cancer. Her loved one survived.

My aunt also tells of a compelling presence that she believes to have been Andrew, who was there while my uncle struggled for his life in an intensive care unit of the hospital. My uncle's cancerous lung had been removed, a surgery from which many go on to lead full lives. But he had not been able to bounce back. In fact, he hung near death. We all prayed. Duane and I especially prayed for Andrew to be there with him. My uncle remained mostly unconscious. He no longer recognized family members. My aunt went to his bedside one morning, and he did not even recognize his wife of nearly fifty years. As she went to sit on the bed at his feet, he struggled to sit up and became quite upset, saying, "Don't sit there!" She asked him why. "Don't sit on the little boy." What little boy, she asked. "Don't you see him? He has been sitting there with me for days." She moved away, and my uncle was very relieved. She knew that Andy was with them, and it filled her with love and hope.

In another case, a St. Matthew's parishioner whose daughter hung near death from a rare, swift, and often fatal heart disease, called upon Andrew to intervene to heal her daughter. It was our grief counselor, Carole. She did not know if her daughter would survive. As she stood in the hospital looking at her daughter breathing shallowly, lips cracked and bleeding, Carole removed a picture of Andrew from her purse and placed it on her daughter's chest. Carole prayed for Andrew to ask Christ to heal her daughter. She later called me and asked me to do the same. "I prayed to Andrew, but I don't know if he heard me. I know he will listen to you. You are his mother." I prayed that day and throughout the next three weeks. Carole's daughter lived, but the doctors were not sure whether her heart or liver had been permanently damaged. Tests could not be administered for three weeks. When the tests were given, there were no signs of damage. She recovered completely.

12

Andrew Holding Up The Sky

With the grief of Christmas behind us, we now faced New Year's Eve. Others around us prepared to celebrate the coming of a new year, but for us, a year without our son was no occasion for any kind of celebration. The coming year, whose prospect already seemed like an eternity, would be the first full calendar year in which we would be forced to live with nothing associated with Andrew except our grief-bound memory. We wept bitterly as midnight approached. Once again, we had to let go—this time we let go of the year that marked our son's sixth birthday and his death.

Thus dawned 1994, a year of certain horror without Andrew, but it was not one without expectation. We awaited word from St. Vladimir's Orthodox Seminary about our application for admission. In mid-January, the call arrived. The seminary faculty wanted to know if they could meet with us during the period from February 2nd through the 4th. The latter date is our son's birthday. Initially, we greeted this news with inner turmoil. How could we visit St. Vladimir's on the date of our son's first birthday after his death? We felt that the day should be spent in mourning and doing charitable works, not discussing our future.

Then we asked ourselves why, of all the dates on the calendar, was February 4th included? No one at the seminary knew that this was Andy's birthday. Because we no longer believed in coincidence, we responded to that call affirmatively, asking God for the strength to do what two grieving parents could not do alone. We were beginning to perceive dimly that it was not at all a fortuitous thing that we should be called on this date. If this were to be the course of our future, then it was all the more fitting that it should be bound up with an anniversary of such significance for us.

I had been preparing myself mentally to quit my government job for the three years we would need to spend at the seminary in New York. The thought of no longer being a career woman and of not having a steady income frightened me. I was ready to explore my identity in Christ and to live for Him. Our bereavement counselor, Carole, said that she did not think I should lose my son and my job in the same year, and that perhaps she knew someone who could help me to get a transfer to New York City for the anticipated duration of our stay at the seminary. I was sceptical of that possibility, to say the least. Federal government downsizing and lean economic times did not bode well for any type of transfer. I prepared myself to scrub floors at McDonald's if necessary to support my family.

Following our bereavement counselor's advice, I took my resume to an associate she had recommended, and told him about my professional background. He seemed genuinely interested and said that he would call his contacts in New York. I thought he was just trying to be polite. I did not put much hope in the prospect, although I did allow myself to discuss the possibility. After waiting several weeks to get a call from him, I left a message with his secretary giving him the dates of our upcoming visit to St. Vladimir's in New York. Still, I heard nothing, and I believed that I never would.

We prepared for our trip. I began thinking in earnest about what job I would be able to get in the city. Gathering my things together on my last day at work before leaving for our interviews, I slipped on my coat, and said goodbye to everyone. They wished me luck,and as I began walking toward the door, I heard a coworker calling to me, "Sandy, the phone is for you. Will you take one last call?" I thought, "Why not?" and picked up the telephone. It was my contact. "You have an interview in New York on February 4th."

We arrived at St. Vladimir's the next day, which coincided with the feast of the Presentation of the Lord in the Temple and the annual Father Alexander Schmemann Memorial Lecture—thus there were no classes scheduled that day. It was an awesome occasion for our first entry into the seminary community. The next two days sped quickly by as we attended chapel, visited members of the seminary faculty, and discussed our plans for the future. Father Thomas Hopko listened to us as we told him some of the story of Andrew's life. He said, "Well, it sounds like we might have a saint on our hands." When he spoke those words, I felt a rush of joy. Andrew's life and death carried much meaning and power. I believed that it should be shared with others. Yet I was afraid. Afraid to share these intimate details of our

lives and afraid that people would think it was all a lie. Listening to
Father Tom, I once again began to feel a tremendous sorrow. He
went on to speak about how one meaningful book can change lives
and contribute to the salvation of thousands of people. I stopped listening. I only wanted to hold my son in my arms.

Andrew's birthday arrived. We began the day by praying for
him in the seminary chapel. Then I made my way by train into Man-
hattan for my interview. I met my prospective employer, and discussed my ideas with him. He was very busy, and had to cut our interview short. Apologizing for rushing me, he stood and said,
"Look, I'll tell you right now you have the job for as long as you want
it." We agreed to arrange the details through my superiors, and I departed. On the train ride back to St. Vladimir's I fought to maintain
my composure because I felt like bursting into tears. The one thing
that we really needed to begin packing for the seminary was a steady
job. I had just been handed one on a silver platter. Such a gift on my
son's birthday! I could not even imagine that this was really happening, yet I felt a twinge of resentment. How could I ever spend Andy's
birthday completely mourning him when God had given us such
hope on that day? I wanted to wallow in my misery and self-pity.
This gift from God kept me from drowning in it.

We returned from that initial trip to St. Vladimir's on a cloud.
Duane and I talked about when to give our notice. I had to talk immediately to my superiors in order to arrange the transfer to New York. I
began the negotiations for my transfer my first day back to work.
Thank God for everyone there who supported me and did not think
that I was out of my mind. The transfer was a miracle because in the
government bureaucracy few things happen in response to an individual's needs. I needed to go to New York to be with my husband and
child. We needed to be at the seminary. Thanks be to God that our
needs coincided with the needs of the government. My superiors saw
the potential value of putting me in New York. After some negotiations
over resource and policy considerations, permission was granted.

To us, this was another indication that this seminary move was
to be; God wanted us there. We also believe that this decision to
send me to New York proved the value of my work, not only to the
government, but to those with whom I worked who benefited from
knowing Andrew through us. When people in pain and need saw

how we continued to live our lives, praising God even without our son, wonderful things happened for them. Some marriages were reconciled, other couples decided to go back to church, some forgave people that they had held grudges against for years. Most people who knew us who had children, thanked God for their blessing and decided to spend a little more time with them and love and protect them to the best of their ability.

The richness of Andrew's life in Christ, his death, and the way we lived our lives through the grace of God and the upholding of the Church also helped attract people to Orthodoxy, beginning with the very first Chistmas after Andy died. Many loving people invited us to Christmas functions, and it was extremely difficult for us. We didn't really want to participate in many parties, but there was one invitation to a Christmas party that I did accept. It was from a group of old friends of mine with whom I had worked upon first being hired by the government. We developed solid, lasting personal relationships that had withstood job changes and all the traumas of our personal lives. We truly cared and continue to care for each other, and they demonstrated the depth of their love for me at this party, which was held at a Greek restaurant in Baltimore. After everyone had eaten and spoken about their Christmas plans, and as we sat sipping coffee, they turned to me and said, "Sandy, how are you? This must be hard for you." They asked how I was doing, what I was feeling, and how I was surviving, particularly after my grandmother's murder. This was unlike many of the other Christmas celebrations I had attended where Andy's name was not even mentioned.

I talked with them about the power of prayer and our church community. I shared my belief that prayer and the community held us together in the hands of God. We could not and have not survived alone. Sometimes I am amazed that I am walking and talking and that we are going forward. People say things like, "Sandy, you are so strong!" But I am not. I alone am helpless. I can do nothing by myself. Prayer and the love of people like the ones I was having lunch with gave us the will to live. They also asked what was happening with regard to the trial of my grandmother's murderer. They showed their love for me by wanting to hear those kinds of details at a Christmas luncheon. I appreciated them asking and being able to talk about it instead of keeping it bottled up inside like a pressure cooker.

After talking about my faith, my church, and our priest who saw us through our darkest hours, we moved on to other topics. Darlene, a women I had not worked with directly but was now part of our group, later pulled me aside and said, "Sandy, can I ask you a question about your religion?"

"Sure," I answered.

"Do you have to be Greek to be Orthodox?" she asked.

I laughed. My original, mistaken conception of Orthodoxy had returned to haunt me. I apologized for laughing and explained the issue of ethnicity to her and how I myself had once believed that you had to be born Orthodox or had to be some other religion. I assured her that ethnicity had nothing to do with true Orthodoxy and told her how much my husband, a convert to Orthodoxy himself, had taught me. I invited her to come to church with us and meet Father Ray, and she did. On that Pascha, she became Orthodox, and I was her sponsor. It was such an exciting moment for me to help bring her into the church, knowing that it had been made possible in part through Andrew's death. Duane and I were blessed the following year by acting as godparents for Darlene and Tom's son, Joshua, a new sprout in the tree of the Church. We marveled at the mysterious chain of events that set all of this into motion. We did not plan, and could not have planned these events. But they let us know that God is God, and a new generation of Orthodoxy is born in hope and love. Faith gives us such relationships, even among friends who are not Orthodox, for when we love, we are one in Christ.

After the holidays, we gave ourselves plenty of time to prepare for the move to the seminary, which was to take us away from the city in which our son was born, raised, and died. I divided up many of Andy's belongings and sent them to relatives for safekeeping since we did not have room to take them all to the seminary with us. As we dismantled Andy's world, our hearts were also torn apart. Duane took pictures of Andy's bedroom before we began the painful process of dismantling it. He also went outside and took photographs of "Andy's world": the playground where Andy ran and shouted, the trails he had blazed through the woods, and other places that were special to them. While packing Andy's room, we found many lost or forgotten Andy "treasures" that would send us into a fit of tears or moaning. I found a little Halloween decoration Andy had made and hung inside the bottom bunk bed still hanging by that piece of tape he had used to secure it. It hurt to put my hand where his once was and remove his artwork.

The entire packing project made us physically sick, but as the boxes began to fill, and our house looked less and less like our home, a strange sense of detachment gripped us. Our nervousness and excitement about the move mounted as we took all the final steps necessary to depart from Maryland. We closed our bank accounts, said our goodbyes, and gave thanks to all who had helped and loved us. We fervently prayed for the strength to walk out of the door for the last time. During all this preparation, thoughts of the truck driver who had hit us that February morning bothered me. I did not want to leave until he knew that we were going forward with our lives and did not blame him for the death of our son. I asked Duane to look at the accident report, which we kept with Andy's death certificate, and get the name and address of the truck driver so that we could get his phone number. Luckily, it was not unlisted. I called one night, and one of his grown children answered the phone. When I explained who I was, they begged me to call back since their father was away for a few days. "Promise that you will," they pleaded.

Two days later, I called, and the truck driver answered the phone. I explained who I was. He drew his breath in and remained silent. I told him that we had all healed physically after the accident and were fine and that Ariana was growing and doing well. Then I explained that we were leaving for the seminary. We did not want to go without letting him know that we did not blame him for our son's death.

The truck driver was in deep emotional pain. "If only I had not been delivering bread on a Sunday, this never would have happened," he finally said.

"And if only I had refused to let anyone go to church, and if only it had not been snowing, ..." I answered him. "We are not in control of all these events. Sometimes things happen just because they are supposed to. I can't explain or understand it . But if we don't blame ourselves and are not blaming you, then you shouldn't blame yourself either."

He thanked me and told me how badly he felt. He said he had wanted to contact us and to attend Andy's funeral. His company's attorney's would not let him, fearing that his showing any remorse for Andy's death would lead us to sue the company. Then he asked a question that to this day brings great sadness to my heart for him, "Where is your son buried?" He had been combing the local cemeteries, looking for my Andy, trying to tell him that he was sorry. I explained that Andy had been buried in Ohio, our home. We said our goodbyes, blessed by the offering of forgiveness.

We then departed Maryland for our new lives, not knowing quite what to expect. I remember arriving at the seminary. I was unsure of myself and did not know how to behave. We felt unworthy of this life, guilty that Andy was not here to share it with us. We moved into our apartment in the married student housing. The semester's classes and the liturgical cycle began to unfold. We stepped into this life, which was to serve a vehicle for our transformation. Our seminary life held great beauty and meaning, but, as in any venture, there was some disappointment along the way. I had arranged for us to begin seeing a grief counselor in New York to help ease our transition to the seminary. When we arrived in September, the counselor was not available. I took this very personally and felt rejected and miserable. Then began innumerable phone calls to Carole in Maryland, trying to find someone in New York with whom we could continue working through our grief. I resented the fact that "Sandy's plan" had not worked out. This was the beginning of my learning the lesson that when God closes a door, He opens a new window of opportunity much greater then anything I could have planned.

This window did not open for us until December when I received an excited call from Carole. "Do you remember the Stephen Daniel Jeffries Foundation?" she asked. Of course I did. Stephen's father, a psychologist, created the foundation in his son's memory after his young son died from leukemia. I had also met Stephen's mother one night at a Compassionate Friends meeting at which she was the guest speaker. "I have a referral for you," Carole continued. "This man was the one with whom Dr. Jeffries chose to work through Stephen's death." As I took down the name, Dr. Gregg Furth, and his Central Park West address, my heart sank. I knew that we could not afford this, and I told Carole so. "Just go," she advised. "Tell him about yourselves and your financial situation, and see what happens."

I phoned Gregg immediately, told him a bit about us, including our inability to pay. Without so much as pausing, he offered us an appointment the very next week. As soon as I heard his soothing voice, full of acceptance and love, I knew that he was the perfect therapist for us. Imagine our surprise as we walked into his office and learned that he was a graduate of our own alma mater, Ohio State University, as well as of the Jung Institute in Switzerland. We needed Gregg's help desperately because, much to our surprise, we found the second year after Andrew's death much more difficult to live through than the first. Much of that first year was spent in shock, but during the second year, each day we discovered a new way in which we missed Andrew. We felt the deep pain of knowing that we could not kiss him or wipe his nose. It was unbearable at times. Gregg helped guide us past many dark abysses in which we could have spent the rest of our entire lives: blame, hatred, and self-pity.

He spoke soothingly about the "synchronicity" of Andrew's death; that it had happened and that it was beyond our control, and that it was an event filled with meanings and connections that were still revealing themselves to us. "If you had known that Andrew would die, would you have gotten into the car that day?" he asked. Of course not, we responded. "Then if you didn't know, you can't be responsible for his death. Not only is it presumptuous, but it's also a selfish thing trying to make yourself responsible, anyhow. It is bigger than you are." I was struck by the "Orthodoxy" of his advice.

Although Duane and I were both very satisfied by the progress we were making in giving meaning to Andrew's death and our suffering, it was not until a few months later that we learned God's plan in bringing us into contact with Gregg. That particular afternoon, I was telling Gregg how I had known from the day I brought Andrew home from the hospital that he would not grow up to be a man, and I told him that Andrew knew, too. "How do you know that?" he asked. I told him about the picture Andrew drew of his death. Gregg grew very still, looking first at me, then at Duane. "Did you know that I have written a book about children who have drawn similar pictures?" he asked. We did not, and all sat quietly in the moment of true discovery.

Gregg rose and took out a copy of his book, "The Secret World of Drawings: Healing Through Art" and presented us with it.[1] We

1 Gregg M. Furth, *The Secret World of Drawings: Healing Through Art*, Introduction by Elisabeth Kuebler-Ross (Massachusetts: Sigo Press, 1988).

agreed to bring in Andrew's pictures the next time so that we could discuss and understand the meaning of them. At the next session, I asked Gregg for a copy of his dissertation, on which he had based the book. I continued my reading, attempting to understand as much of Andrew's drawings as possible without having Andrew himself there to explain them to us. After reading and discussing these works, I took out every one of Andrew's drawings. To my surprise, we found more than one indication that he, at least at the unconscious level, knew of his death and future life in Christ.

I'll begin by describing the most obvious examples of Andrew's knowledge, the Sunday-school picture he drew of his own death. When I collected my thoughts on this picture, I phoned his Sunday-school teacher to ask for any additional details that might help me. She explained that following the lesson about St. Stephen, the children were asked to draw a picture of this saint. Andy drew the scene of the accident, with himself lying alongside the road with two stones sailing toward him with a full sun blazing in the sky. He combined the elements of his death with that of St. Stephen. That much we already knew before even meeting Gregg, but talking with him and reading his book gave us further insight. One piece of advice he gave us was always to look at the back of the picture to see if there are any additional details. Duane and I found something else on the back of this particular picture. It is a drawing of the wreckage of the car, exactly like the one he drew of the scene of the accident, with one exception. This time Andy is not beside the road. He is ascending into the sky. He drew a line between himself, the car, and three heads that remained at the scene, Duane, Ariana, and myself.

The colors that Andy used to draw these pictures are also important. He had his choice of any color of crayon or marker. He made his picture completely in red, the color of martyrdom.

He drew his picture on yellow paper, framing the red of martyrdom in the light of the life-giver. Our attention to color and meaning also led us to look carefully at the cover of Andy's notebook, which he filled with orange and green scribbles. Perhaps, if he had been able to articulate his intuitions, he might have been able to tell us what these scribbles depicted. But today, with the knowledge of his death, it almost looks like a flashing green and orange light, saying, "Warning, Warning." The dark green coloring suggests health and growth, while the orange could forecast a life or death struggle. Combining these elements, we can say that he saw his death as an opportunity for growth.

When we looked through all of Andy's drawings, searching for other pictures of the accident or other possible forecasting pictures, we found three more significant drawings. Each one was made in the last six months of his life. One particularly haunting drawing is one of those he made in Kindergarten with Miss Codd. She often asked the children to draw a picture of whatever they wanted. When they were finished, she would ask them what the picture represented and would write it on the picture for the parents to understand. This picture is drawn on pink construction paper and is entitled "Andrew Holding Up the Sky." In it, Andrew is very tall, with very long arms raised up to the sky. Smiling, yet showing signs of the responsibility of this burden, Andrew has no real lower body, only a torso that looks like a robe. This Andrew is drawn in simple stick figure form and is a pale blue, so pale that he can barely be seen. He holds up a light purple sky that also contains a blazing sun, Andy's trademark, my child of the light. Duane and I spent some time talking about this picture and its meaning. Then he turned to me and said, "Who holds up the sky?"

"God does," I answered.

Duane continued, "I think this picture shows that Andrew has ascended to God, and with all that, the sun is still shining."

Finally, we found a picture Andrew had made on his own at home, one of his many evening projects. This drawing is on a large piece of cardboard box, and looks as though Andy was making a postcard. On the side where the address would appear, he drew six smiling faces, and then put an X through each of them; then he drew the number 7 with no face. To us, this means Andrew crossed out each of the years of his life and put the number 7, with no human depiction, possibly because, on some level, he understood that he would not know that number in earthly terms.

Although working with Gregg and trying to understand these drawings helped give us some closure to Andrew's death, these little glimmers of hope and understanding sometimes became swallowed up by larger issues that we faced, or tried to avoid—such as putting a headstone on Andy's grave. More than a year after Andy's death, his

Andrew holding up the sky

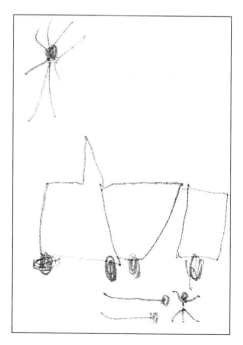

Andrew's premonition:
the scene of the accident.

grave still had no headstone. I could not bear to see his name on a slab of granite with the date of his birth and death. That was too real, too final for me. Anytime my poor mother tried to approach me on the subject, I lashed out, asking to be left alone. I was not about to go tombstone shopping.

In a quieter moment, my father asked me how I envisioned Andy's stone. I told him that I believed that one day people would come to see this child in order to pray, seek healing and understanding. I thought that his grave should be a place of prayer and should look like a little chapel. "What if I designed something like that for you?" he asked. I looked at him in amazement and agreed. My father went to work on it, found a contractor, and soon had plans for us to see. The design is simple yet beautiful, a single large stone for the entire six-grave plot, with a fully sculpted Orthodox cross carved out of its center and framed in an arch, forming a personal prayer niche at the cemetery. We had purchased the plot not only for our son's burial but also for our own and for that of my parents; we also included a single unnamed grave. All of our names and dates of birth are inscribed on the stone. That comforted me greatly. Andrew was not alone, my name stood beside his, in anticipation of the day on which the Lord would choose to lay me next to my baby. This gave me greater direction and strength, knowing that the pain of this world would all pass away, and that God willing, one day we would all be together. Andrew's death produced this strength in us. We knew that after burying him, we could bury anyone.

It was Duane's wish that we select a verse to put on the stone, a verse that would serve as a summation of all that we believe. It was after some searching that he came upon this verse from St. Paul's First Epistle to the Corinthians: "For as in Adam all die; so in Christ all will be made alive." (15:22 NIV) We chose this verse because it expresses what is surely the most fundamental Christian conviction—that we who have heard and received the gospel have no choice but to live with the one hope that is born from it. Our bondage to death has been broken only because we, the foolish, helpless creatures that we are, have chosen to live shielded by the hope of Christ. It is a hope that we came to see our son embrace, in the simple, direct and probably instinctive way that only a six year-old child would know.In June of 1994, Father Ray Velencia and his family traveled from Maryland to Ohio to bless Andrew's grave and headstone. We gathered together

on the top of the hill, and with some members of the Holy
Resurrection Serbian Orthodox Church choir from Steubenville sang
"Memory Eternal." We cried, tears of sorrow, but not despair. We
huddled together, physically and emotionally supporting each other
during the service that morning. At the conclusion of the service a
church bell began to ring. The sun broke through the dark clouds
which had been threatening rain. Birds flew chirping around us.
Father Ray looked quizically in my direction and later asked me if I
had arranged for someone to ring the bell at that moment. I had not.

13

Open To Love And Eternal
Transformation

Having written all this about Andrew's life, death, burial, and the blessing of his monument, one might think that I could say, "And they all lived happily ever after." But this is not a fairy tale. Even before the blessing of our son's grave, the spiritual warfare over writing this book had already begun. I do not think that this work would be complete without describing the process of writing the book, as well as the profound and transformational effect that seminary life and Andy's death had on us all.

I began writing seven months after Andrew died. I knew that I had to complete an outline to be certain that I would not forget any important details. In the evenings after Ariana went to bed, I would go into Andrew's bedroom, switch on the computer and outline each phase of his life. There were already a number of things that I knew would have to be included in the book. It was only after I began to think in terms of an overall outline that many other events came forward to be included. During this process, I would ask people for input, particularly my husband and the parishioners at St. Matthew's. Before leaving for the seminary in August of 1994, the outline was nearly completed.

Our arrival at the seminary and my new job did not initially dissuade me from work on the book. Eventually, however, I began losing ground in what was to become for me a pitched spiritual battle. I listened to negative thoughts that told me, "This is far too private. What will people think?" Or to even more damning thoughts like, "People will call you a liar. Some people will even question your motives for writing the book. They will think that you are either crazy or puffed up with pride, or both." These thoughts took up far too much time and attention in my head. Suddenly I could not find the strength to write. It was only gradually that I came to realize that it was not yet time. First, I had to understand what had happened to us, and then I had to allow myself to be transformed by it.

Our journey to the seminary included great loss. Whole sections of what we had been until that time were amputated. When we came to the first day of orientation at the seminary, Duane and I sat clutching each other's hands in the basement of the chapel. We sat there in the second or third row, and the faculty of St. Vladimir's spoke about what was expected of us as new seminarians and what seminary life was about. The Dean stood before us and said that we had to be broken down for any change to take place. If we were not broken and refashioned before we left the seminary, then there was indeed a very good chance that something had gone wrong along the way. I began to cry. I could not imagine being any more broken than I already was. "God, just leave me alone," I thought, "these people just don't know what we've been through." The Dean of Students also spoke to the orientation group saying, "You are in this community now. Be a part of it. Don't be tempted to be off to this thing and the other. Be a part of us."

Going into that first year, I did not take the advice of allowing myself to be further broken, or of really being in the community. I tried to do things according to my will and my desires. And of course, it did not work very well because it was not the will of God. It was simply my will. I was trying to decide, without His help, what was right and what I should do. Being a working wife I felt the stress of working long hours. I would then come home and try to do everything that the non-working seminary wives did. I thought I had to do this in order to prove that I could be a priest's wife, too. This was not who God called me to be. I was making my decisions based on what people would think or say (as if I had any control over that) and that is inevitably a recipe for some form of living hell.

The sheer energy I expended in trying to be what I thought other people expected me to be is what crushed and broke me by the end of that first year. I gradually began to see that I had to set limits and boundaries. I had to discover who I was called to be in Christ, the seminary community and in my work. I slowly realized that I could not do all of the seemingly countless things that were now being placed in my path because—and this is always the most difficult truth for any sinner to accept—I was not God. I was only Sandy.

And Sandy is who God created me to be. So, in the wake of this re-luctant realization, and also with the knowledge and power of for-giveness in me, my life began to change.

It was during our first Lent at the seminary that I felt compelled to forgive the man who murdered my grandmother, and especially to forgive his family. I came to feel a deep compassion for them and a sense of shared grief. In having been separated from my son, I knew some of the pain they felt in being separated from theirs. That child was sentenced to life in prison, without parole, to spend the rest of his days in a federal prison. His family is in hell. When he was sentenced, it was one of the only days since Andy died that I could not go to work because I was too emotionally upset. I cried all night and the next day, grieving for his mother.

My sister sent me the newspaper clipping of his sentencing. The front-page story began, "With his mother crying in the background behind him, Scott Howell was sentenced to life." I also grieved for him. What could make this child feel such anger and hatred that he would commit such a heinous act? I felt such pain for all of them, and such forgiveness. I do not condone what he did by any means, but, my God, what pain and emptiness and desolation there must have been in his heart for him to have done such a thing! It was horrifying to contemplate what kind of demonic power there must be, and how it is capable of seizing a poor human soul and erasing its traces of human-ity. And for that, I forgave him and his family. The horror of what he did, and having to live in that small town, must be devastating to them, but I want them to know that we do not hate them.

This act of forgiveness in my heart healed me. During that first Lent, I went to confession and crying, told my father confessor about having forgiven the truck driver and also about having for-given the murderer and his family. He nodded his head slowly and said, "That's something good," not quite understanding my point. Sobbing, and barely able to speak, I then confessed that I could not forgive my father. How could I forgive murder and not my own fa-ther? "What has he done?" he asked.

"He never wanted me. He doesn't love me. Nothing I have ever done is good enough," I blurted out before Christ. These were the charges, I am ashamed to say, that I leveled at my father since I could speak. They are charges rooted in my own selfishness and need to control every situation. It is I that never had enough or appreciated anything. In working through my feelings, I began to understand the self-destructive role that my own pride-filled ego had played in my life. My father confessor helped me see that I was the problem, not my father. During confession, he led me to talk about my problem with food. I told him that even during Lent, I was not eating meat, but was eating huge quantities of the food that is permitted. I felt terrible. But in admitting that I had a problem, I could begin to see my obsession and compulsion, and my sins. My best thinking had inflated me to nearly three hundred pounds again. By God's grace, with Father Tom's guidance, and the help of several support groups, I stopped my compulsive overeating.

The people who participated in this fellowship understood food as a drug, as the focus of compulsive behavior. By putting down the food, I was able to understand that it is not God's will for me to weigh almost three hundred pounds. That had been Sandy's will run amok. It was my ego that had ballooned itself up to three hundred pounds. Me, me, me, and what I wanted, what I needed—that had been my rule of life. I was sick of myself and felt as though I were drowning in it. With my new eating plan, I was able to taste a new kind of freedom. I prayed for Christ to accompany me. In this way I came to know Him and His merciful, saving power to a degree that I had never even dreamed possible.

Over the next year, God took nearly one hundred and twenty-five pounds from me. God's will said that I did not need that extra baggage anymore. My body was transformed. More importantly, my spirit was also transformed. The problems that I had had in all the relationships in my life—all of the accumulated resentment, anger and frustration of the past, I was able to lay at God's feet. I begged Him to take it from me. That burden weighed far more than the pounds that I was losing. God was merciful, and He took this burden from me. All of this began to happen after I admitted my role in what had been my life up until that time—I was not a victim, I had not been dealt a rotten hand. There was really nothing to resent. There was only my life and the way I had chosen to live it. How I lived had not been forced upon me, I chose it freely, in the same unfortunate way that every sinner comes to participate in his own personal undoing. It was only after I faced this painful truth about myself that I was able to move forward. What I did, I did not do alone; in the end it was only possible with God's help. I could never have done it on my own, and cannot continue to do it on my own because now I understand that alone, I am nothing. Alone I am left in hell.

Through prayer, forgiveness, and love I came closer to being a whole person, fully human, as God had created me to be. I still fell into real temptation and thought at one point that I could stop sinning, but I could never stop. I would do writings, readings, and go to confession, thinking that I could purge myself completely and at last be done with it. But every morning, I woke up fallen and human, and still Sandy. And I learned that the best I can do is to try to be better, not try to be God.

Through my healing, I was able to continue the work of finishing this book, not only out of a sense of obligation, but as a gift freely given. How many times over the year that I struggled and lost the battle to work on this book did I hear those words I first heard while laying in Baltimore's shock trauma unit—"You must not let this life pass unnoticed. You must write a book."

Fear had its stranglehold on me. I was afraid to continue writing, lest people should think I was deluded. I was even more afraid about what some people were beginning to say about Andrew—that he was a saint. I thought that if he was a saint, then he would not be mine anymore, he would belong to all the people. I began to have nightmares. In one particularly vivid one, Andrew was declared a saint. His body was exhumed and the coffin was placed on the table with the bagels during coffee hour after church on Sunday. That dream cost me many months of work. I did not want to have anything more to do with this book.

It took me a year to pull myself far enough out of the slavery of my own reasoning to continue working. Without my recovery, God's help and the prayers of many, this book would never have been completed. I began my writing sessions in front of a picture of Andrew in his altar boy's robe and my triptych of Christ, Mary and John the Baptist, by lighting a candle and praying. One prayer, from a "Prayer Book for Orthodox Christians," helped me greatly.[1] The

---

1 "Prayer Book for Orthodox Christians," compiled by the Very Rev. Dr. Mateja Matejic (Columbus, OH: Kosovo Publishing Company, 1990).

prayer asks, "Almighty God, our Help and Refuge, the Fountain of Wisdom and Tower of Strength, Who knowest that I can do nothing without Thy guidance and help: assist me, I pray Thee, and direct me to divine wisdom and power, that I may accomplish this task, and whatever I may undertake to do, faithfully and diligently, according to Thy will, so that it may be profitable to myself and others, and to the glory of Thy Holy Name. For Thine is the Kingdom, and the Power, and the Glory, of the Father, and of the Son, and of the Holy Spirit, now and ever, and unto ages of ages. Amen"

I also prayed to the *Theotokos*.[2] I feel very close to her. She knows my pain, for her heart was also pierced with the sword of grief. She held the body of her dead son in her arms and lamented. I ask her to help me repeat her faith and embrace my life saying, "Let it be unto me, as you have said."

I was not the only person in my family transformed by our life at St. Vladimir's. My husband blossomed after that first year. He had found his true calling and identity in Christ. I was amazed at the impact it had on his behavior. I would hear him outside the married student housing talking to people and laughing. I would think, "Is that my husband? The person who would barely say six words to my coworkers?" He had always prefered to stay on the sidelines of life because he believed that he had nothing of value to offer people. I once asked him why he would not talk when we went out to lunch with other couples. He looked at me honestly and said, "I never think that I have anything to say that people would be interested in." He clearly did not believe that anymore.

During his second year, after being ordained a deacon, Duane began preaching from the pulpit, and it was then, if I had not been certain before, that I knew that my husband had been called and was exactly where he belonged. Duane had never been much of a public speaker. It was in Arabic class at Ohio State University that I realized I loved him—before we even had a single date. On this occasion, he was speaking before a group, doing a class assignment in

2 Greek for 'birthgiver of God'. The liturgical title reserved for the Virgin Mary who gave birth to Jesus, the incarnate Word of God. Orthodox Christians often offer prayers, both private and liturgical, to her asking for her intercession before God.

which he was to deliver a mini-lecture to the other students in Arabic. Although his Arabic was impeccable, his face was blood red, he kept pulling nervously at his neck, and the vein in his throat was throbbing. He did not like speaking in front of the class. When I saw his discomfort, I immediately wanted to protect him. I felt a rush of love for him.

These memories of Duane's public speaking struck fear in my heart when it was time for him to begin giving sermons at St. Vladimir's. He was scheduled to deliver his first sermon one morning at Matins. After Duane wrote it, I asked him to practice by giving it to me, remembering the man with the red face, uncomfortable and uncertain of himself in front of the Arabic class. I was afraid of what he might do in front of the chapel, and I asked him to recite it for me. He refused, saying, "There is no practice. I give this from the *amvon*."[3]

The next morning I went into church with some anxiety, fearing that his sermon would not be good, or even heard. But my husband delivered an incredibly beautiful and moving sermon that even brought some people to tears. He delivered it calmly, clearly, and distinctly. Again I thought, "Is that my husband?" I was so awed by the power of God and the power of love and faith and its ability to transform people and their lives. Duane said he was not alone in giving that sermon. He felt Andrew was there, too.

Ariana has also been blessed by our life at the seminary. To explain this, I need to examine in more depth, the relationship she had with Andrew before he died, and her own journey of grief. Seminary life cushioned her grief because of the presence of other children in our married student housing complex. We had Ariana so that we could have children to raise together. Suddenly after Andy's death, she was alone. Andrew and Ariana had an incredibly close relationship as brother and sister, particularly given that the relationship began from birth and was so strong that even after Andrew died when Ariana was only nine months old, she has never forgotten him and contines to grieve his passing. When Ariana was only three months old, they began playing together. In the mornings, I would get Ariana out of her crib, change her, and then carry her to the top bunk

---

3 The elevated area in front of the icon screen. It is customary for an Orthodox priest to stand here while either delivering a homily or addressing the people.

where Andy lay sleeping. I would then place her in his arms, and she would begin grabbing him. He would wake up laughing. They loved these mornings so much. Andy was with Ariana for most of the day at the sitters. He was proud of her and very protective. At home in the evening, I would be fixing dinner, and he would take her in his room and shut the door. I worried that she would put something in her mouth. But her brother had the situation under control and did not want to be disturbed. He simply shut the door. They were together in their world. I quit worrying. He always wanted to carry her and care for her. They were very much a part of each other's lives. He had some twinges of jealousy and wanted to sit on me when I was feeding her, and my lap was big enough for two.

When Andy died, Ariana could not understand what was happening. At the scene of the accident, she was unconscious. I did not take her to the viewings at the funeral home and did not take her to the funeral. It was too much for me. I was afraid that she would try to call him out of the coffin to play with her. After we returned to Maryland, she crawled into Andy's room, stopped, pointed at the top bunk and sputtered, "Br..Br..." She wanted her brother. How could I explain to her where her brother was? Her tiny grief broke my heart.

Ariana missed her brother and remembered him. I would tell people that she pointed and asked for him. She would go to his pictures and carry them to me asking for him. People told me that she would forget him. I knew that once she began talking, she would ask for him.

One Sunday, I stayed home from church because I was ill. Ariana sat playing in the living room, and I layed on the couch with a blanket over me watching her. She stopped and turned to me and asked, "Where is Andy?" And I froze. How do you explain to a one year-old that her brother is dead? "Andy is with God, Ariana. Andy died," I told her. She continued to ask questions over the next two years. "When are we going to see him?" I told her only God knows the time when we willl see each other again. "If he is with God, why won't you let him come home?" I told her he is home. Our true home is with God. One day we would all be there together. "Can we go and see him?" she asked.

We used Andy's bunkbeds for Ariana when she outgrew her crib. The bunkbeds were intended to be for both our children. We saw no reason to get rid of them and buy Ariana something else. She uses his books and the toys that are appropriate for her age. They share everything. She talks about her brother. One afternoon a short while after turning two, she was looking at the picture of Andy and herself that we have hanging in our living room, and said, "Andy is my brother." I assured her that it was true and asked her what she remembered about her brother. I expected to hear her repeat a story about Andy that I might have told her. Instead she turned to me smiling and said, "Remember in the swimming pool when Andy used to pop up and scare me?"

I drew my breath in shock. No, I had not remembered that at all, until that moment. Ariana was describing a scene at the swimming pool. She could not have been more than three months old at the time. She was born in May, and during swimming season that summer, we would take her and Andy to the pool. I would sit on the edge of the pool with her on my lap. Andy would swim in the water with his snorkel set that his Baba had bought for him. He would pop up out of the water yelling, "Peek-a-boo!" Ariana would giggle. They would do it over and over again. She thought he was so funny. And this is what my daughter told me. Having her tell me something I did not remember was a shock and frightening to me. I asked Duane how she could possibly remember these things, and Duane simply said, "Because she is supposed to."

Today, at four years, Ariana remains confused, and upset at times, about Andy's death, especially when people say that she does not have any brothers or sisters. She is Andy's sister and wants everyone to know it. She brooded for an entire day once when someone called her an only child. At the dinner table that night after the blessing of the food she declared, "I am a sister, and Andy is my brother." I assured her that would always be true.

Ariana understands a great deal about God and about what we are doing with our lives. One night around Andy's birthday and the time of his death, I was feeling very sad. I put Ariana into bed and crawled in beside her to read her the usual bedtime story. She looked at me and asked, "Momma, what is wrong?" I said, "I just feel very sad today, Ariana." She looked at me fully and said, "Sometimes I feel sad, too."

As a result of being at St. Vladimir's, Ariana has also healed. We have healed our relationship with each other. A part of my heart was ripped out when Andrew died. The remaining fragments were afraid to ever love again, lest I lose Ariana, too. Today, I am open to love, but that does not mean that I am free of pain by any means. The pain still remains very physical as well as emotional. When I am feeling deep grief I can develop a migraine headache, cramps, and nausea. There are times when I still feel that Andrew's flesh is being ripped from my body. It is overwhelming. I don't think that will ever end. When I talk about healing and salvation, I mean it as an everyday occurrence.

We have learned to suffer in a positive way. I have learned to suffer through the pain, and have the suffering be to the glory of God, and for the sake of my son's memory. I have learned to distinguish between suffering that is unnecessary because it is born of sin and self-indulgence and the suffering that is unto my salvation and the salvation of others—the "godly sorrow" (2 Cor 7:9, 10). A wise man once told me that whatever you turn to in your time of need is your God. That frightened me because I could see that, in the past, I had turned time and time again, to food in order to fill the emptiness inside me that only communion with God can satisfy.

On September 28, 1996, His Beatitude, Metropolitan Theodosius ordained Deacon Duane Martin to the holy priesthood at St. Luke's Church in McLean, Virginia, on the occasion of the Diocesan Day festival. Priests and parishioners from every parish in the diocese gathered along with our family, relatives, and seminary friends for this blessed event. Duane and I had taken Andy to the Diocesan Day festival before, and being ordained at St. Luke's was very special to us.

Ariana and I received communion from Father Duane Martin first. I looked at the Metropolitan, who was also giving communion. He was standing in the exact spot he had been standing three years earlier when he gave Andy communion. Andy had on a new Ninja Turtle belt that morning. After he received communion, he turned to the Metropolitan and said, "Hey, how do you like my Ninja Turtle belt?" The Metropolitan looked a bit puzzled at first. Then he saw Andy pulling out the belt for him to inspect. He warmly smiled his approval. Andy went away a happy boy.

During the ordination liturgy, the Metropolitan said that in understanding evil we should behave like children, but in all other things we should behave like responsible adults. I carried this message away with me and thought about it a great deal. A few days later while I was out for my morning run, I began to compare myself to someone else, and understanding struck down that comparison. I understood that if I am to behave like an adult, I must leave behind all comparisons to my fellow human beings, for God, the Father of us all, has perfect love for each of us. I do not have to be greater than or less than any of my brothers for God to love me. When I compare, I am a child practicing sibling rivalry! This fuller knowledge of God's love for me, and each of us individually is a gift I received from the ordination.

The full impact of Duane becoming a priest did not completely register until the next day, when, at the Metropolitan's request, he served his first liturgy at St. Matthew's church in Columbia. As Duane stood fully vested between the icons at the altar that my son died to serve, I became conscious of everything that led us to that moment. "Out of the ashes of our lives, this is what has arisen," I thought.

I hope I always remember how grateful I felt at that moment and that I keep my heart open to love and the eternal transformation that embracing God brings. Now I pray to the one and true God for the strength to turn to Him in good times and bad. I thank Him for the opportunity to grow each day. It is with gratitude and joy that I release this work into His loving arms, to the Glory of God the Father. Amen.

Epilogue

Father Duane M. Johnson

To lose a child is the ultimate human tragedy. There is nothing else to surpass it, because this event—the death of a child—violates every last notion by which we live. It runs counter to all of our mortal assumptions, and it leaves all who witness it, even those who experience it from afar, with a profound sense that nature itself has been turned upside down by the untimely passing of one little life. So it was with our son Andrew.

It is a difficult thing to speak about his death. I find that words, and even the thoughts and feelings that precede them, have a way of faltering before the fact. It is a fact that crushed me and my wife, an event that swept away all of our footing, and we fell. We fell until we hit something. We fell until we hit the open arms of Christ. Our Lord was there to receive us, His own suffering children, at what was the moment of our supreme weakness. In those first few days after the accident we called upon His name. He heard our cries. He raised us up from our hospital beds, broken though we were, to stand by our son's coffin so that we might be able to look upon his smooth, gentle face once more.

We did this with the bitterest grief, but there was in the midst of our suffering a mild hope that filled our souls. It was a hope that was born out of the moment—the experience of sitting next to our son's still and lifeless body and simply gazing at his face. It was in that moment that we were seeing his face in eternity. He was dead, but in his death our son was showing something to us. As real as death was, Andrew showed us that even its immovable reality was not ultimate. There was something there more permanent, more enduring, and thus more real. There was love.

But not love as sentiment or bittersweet nostalgia, but rather love as connection, as the fragile but life-giving realization that Andrew was not lost. Our hearts were still connected. The one link now left between us was the most real one of all—that of a love shared in Christ. Our boy was dead, but Sandy and I were to discover that we loved him more than ever, and we knew that he loved us. It is an unbroken, unbreakable connection. We are joined to Andrew by a bond of love. Metropolitan Anthony (Bloom) writes: "We know that everything we possess has been given us by God and is not even ours for ever or with certainty. Everything can be taken away from us except love, and this is what makes love unique and something we can give....love is a gift of God, because we cannot produce it out of ourselves, yet, once we possess it, it is the only thing that we can withold or offer."[1]

But this kind of love does not exist on its own. It has no being apart from the beings who live with it and, by God's grace, in it. It is a grave mistake to imagine that we can think of this love as being something that we can consider abstractly. This love cannot be separated from all of the things that we as individual human beings think, feel, confess, hope, and do. The kind of love to which we are called by Christ is not an abstraction. He has commanded that our love must be what we do.

A love left untried is only an abstraction; the path to a perfect love is not by leaving it untouched in our minds, the proud object of our personal contemplation. But a love that has been spent, one that has been given freely and with no thought of consequence, in short, a love that has been crucified—that is the first step in the direction of perfect love. This is the meaning of Jesus' words when he admonishes us: "You, therefore, must be perfect, as your heavenly Father is perfect." (Matthew 5:48) It is God's everlasting wish that we do love each other, that we should never be afraid to learn how to love, and to be loved by others.

God's perfect love is a trinitarian love, one that is shared. It is in this sense that when we love another person we participate in them. That person becomes for us a living presence, a person indwelling in our consciousness. If we love, then we are never, spiritually speaking, alone. Even if it is a relationship in which there is not a mutual love, that person—the one we love—still participates in us. And, if we pray for those who do not love us, then we are participating mystically in them. This is, as St. Paul reminds us about so much that is involved in the spiritual life, a "great mystery." God is calling us to look at the world with transfigured eyes, with a vision that sees beyond the immediate, to what is lasting, to what it is that reveals God's own presence

1 Metropolitan Anthony of Sourozh, *Living Prayer*, p. 14.

in this world. Love brings us into the presence of God, a presence that sanctifies and heals those who taste of its sweetness. We as Christians have to discover what it means to become a student of love. It belongs to us to submit to love's lessons. All is not obvious, for there is much to learn. Loving is God's own challenge to each of us. Love, as Metropolitan Anthony says, comes from God and it is the one thing that we are free to give and to receive.

This is what we require for the spiritual life, for a life spent walking in pursuit of God's "perfect law" (James 2:25): we need to see that it is, above all else, a way of love. The Christian life is one spent reckoning with love's implications. To that end we learn that we require faith. But faith is not something with which we begin our journey. It is rather something that we acquire along the way, an outlook that comes after we have absorbed the bitter truths of love's way and its even deeper consolations. We walk by faith, a step at a time, until the end. Faith ends up being a record of the love that we receive and give in this life, from and to God and each other.

Sandy and I weep over our son. His body is no longer here. The hand that we held, the face that we kissed, these things belong to the earth for the time being. Now we live with what lingers in our hearts. What remains for us is the love, our boy's gift to us. In our eyes he is the perfect son, our only son. He speaks to us of God.

Appendix

From the Funeral Service of the Holy Orthodox Church for a Child

Troparia

O only Creator, who with profound wisdom mercifully orders all things, and gives unto all that which is useful: Give rest, O Lord, to the soul of Thy servant who is fallen asleep. For (he, she) has placed (his, her) trust in Thee, our Maker and Fashioner, and our God.

Glory to the Father, and to the Son, and to the Holy Spirit, now and ever and unto ages of ages. Amen.

We have you as a bulwark and a haven, and an intercessor well-pleasing to God, Whom you have borne, O Virgin Birthgiver of God—the salvation of the faithful.

Canon
Ode 3

O Lord, Builder of the vault of heaven, and Founder of the Church, as You are our supreme desire and the Support of the faithful, confirm me in love of You, Who alone are the love of mankind.

Reader: Give rest, O Lord, to this child who is fallen asleep.

O Truly-perfect Word, who revealed yourself as a perfect infant: You have translated to Yourself this child who has not seen adulthood. Give rest to him (her) with all the righteous who have been well-pleasing to you, O only Lover of mankind.

Reader: Give rest, O Lord, to this child who is fallen asleep.

Show to be a communicant of all heavenly good things this uncorrupted child who had not tasted of nor been enraptured by earthly sweet things, O Compassionate One, who You have translated at Your divine command.

Reader: Glory to the Father, and to the Son, and to the Holy Spirit, now and ever and unto ages of ages. Amen.

Make this most-pure infant whom You have been well-pleased to translate, O Savior, a partaker of the heavenly mansions, of bright repose, and of the sacred choir of the Saints, O Lord.

Sedalion

Truly all things are vanity, and life is but a shadow and a dream. For everyone born of the earth strives in vain, as the Scriptures say. For when we have acquired the world, then do we take up our abode in the grave, where kings and beggars, old men and children lie down together. Therefore, O Christ God, grant rest to Thy servant, this child, departed this life, as the Lover of mankind.

Ode 6

I pour forth my prayer before the Lord and to Him do I make known my sorrows, for my soul has been filled with evil, and my life has been drawn near to Hell. And like Jonah I pray: O God, lead me up from corruption!

Reader: Give rest, O Lord, to this child who is fallen asleep.

As an infant You were laid in a manger and You submitted Yourself to the embrace of the Elder who had begotten infants. Before this child had attained fulness of stature, You have led (him, her) to life. Therefore, with thanksgiving we glorify You.

Reader: Give rest, O Lord, to this child who is fallen asleep.

You cried out to the Apostles: "Suffer the little children to come to me, for to such who are like them in spirit is My Kingdom given." Grant Your light to this child who has been translated to You.

Reader: Glory to the Father, and to the Son, and to the Holy Spirit, now and ever and unto ages of ages. Amen.

You have deprived Your child of earthly good things, that You might make (him, her) to be a partaker of Your heavenly good things, since (he, she) has not transgressed Your divine commandments. We glorify the immeasurable depth of Your justice, O Good One.

Kontakion

With the saints give rest, O Christ, to the soul of Thy servant, where there is neither sickness, nor sorrow nor sighing, but life everlasting.

Oikos

Thou alone art immortal, who has created and fashioned man. For out of the earth were we mortals made, and unto the same earth shall we return again, as Thou commanded when Thou madest me, saying to me: For you are dust and to the dust shall you return. And so to dust all we mortals shall go, making our funeral dirge the song: Alleluia!

No one suffers more than a mother; no one is more touched than a father. For they are troubled when they send forth their children from this life. Great is the pity they have in their hearts for the sake of their children, and yet the more when these are sweet of speech, as they call to remembrance their words with the song: Alleluia!

O God, God who has summoned me: Be the consolation now to my household, for great affliction has fallen upon them. All gaze on me, having me as their only-begotten one. But, You who were born of a Virgin Mother, refresh the womb of my mother, and bedew the heart of my father with this song: Alleluia!

Ode 9

The heavens were afraid and the ends of the earth were awed, for God has appeared to men in the flesh and your womb became more spacious than the heavens. Therefore the orders of men and angels magnify you as Theotokos.

Reader: Give rest, O Lord, to this child who is fallen asleep.

O Christ Who became an infant without change, and Who, of Your own will, joined Yourself to the Cross and looked upon the motherly afflictions of her that bore You: Appease the sorrows and cruel afflictions of the faithful parents of this departed child, that we may glorify Your majesty.

Reader: Give rest, O Lord, to this child who is fallen asleep.

O King of all, having summoned this blessed infant from on high and taking (him, her), like a pure bird, to its heavenly nest, You have saved this soul from many snares, and have united it with the souls of the righteous who are delighting in Your Kingdom.

Reader: Glory to the Father, and to the Son, and to the Holy Spirit, now and ever and unto ages of ages. Amen.

You granted the heavenly abode, O Word of God, to children who have done nothing evil, and likewise You have been well-pleased, O Good One, to number Your creature with them. Console the afflictions of the parents of the child who has now come to You, for You are all-compassionate and the Lover of Mankind.

Holy God, Holy Mighty, Holy Immortal, have mercy on us.
Holy God, Holy Mighty, Holy Immortal, have mercy on us.
Holy God, Holy Mighty, Holy Immortal, have mercy on us.

Glory to the Father, and to the Son, and to the Holy Spirit, now and ever and unto ages of ages. Amen.

Prokeimenon

Reader: Blessed is the way in which you walk today, O soul, for a place of rest has been prepared for you.

The first letter of the Holy Apostle Paul to the Corinthians [15:39-45]:

All flesh is not the same: Men have one kind of flesh, animals have another, birds another and fish another. There are also heavenly bodies and there are earthly bodies; but the splendor of the heavenly bodies is of one kind, and the splendor of the earthly bodies is another. The sun has one kind of splendor, the moon another and the stars another; and star differs from star in splendor. So will it be with the resurrection of the dead. The body that is sown is perishable, it is raised imperishable; it is sown in dishonor, it is raised in glory; it is sown in weakness, it is raised in power; it is sown a natural body, it is raised a spiritual body. If there is a natural body, there is also a spiritual body. So it is written: "The first man Adam became a living being"; the last Adam, a life-giving spirit.

Gospel

Holy Gospel according to Saint John [6:35-40]:

The Lord said to the Jews who came to Him, "I am the bread of life. He who comes to me will never go hungry, and he who believes in me will never be thirsty. But as I told you, you have seen me and still you do not believe. All that the Father gives me will come to me, and whoever comes to me I will never drive away. For I have come down from heaven not to do my will but to do the will of him who sent me. And this is the will of him who sent me, that I shall lose none of all that he has given me, but raise them up at the last day.

Hymn for the Last Kiss

O my child, who would not mourn over your lamentable departure from this life? For as an immature child, quickly as a bird you have flown from your mother's embrace and have fled to the Creator of us all. O my child, who would not weep, beholding your bright countenance, which formerly was beautiful as a rose, now withered.

Death brings release to infants. They were pure of life's wickedness and attained peace. They rejoice with a heavenly joy in the bosom of Abraham, and now they delight with the divine choir of holy innocents, and truly they rejoice, for they departed pure from this sinful corruption.

Glory to the Father, and to the Son, and to the Holy Spirit.

Once Adam tasted from the tree in Eden, and sickness befell him, when the serpent injected its venom, for through it comes the inescapable death which devours man. But the Master of all has come to us, defeating the serpent and giving us repose. Therefore let us cry out to Him: protect and give rest with the saints to the one You have received, O Savior.

Now and ever and unto ages of ages. Amen.

O Virgin Mother of God, Consolation of the sorrowful, Deliverance of the weak, preserve our habitation and people, for you are the Security of the defenseless, Calm of the agitated, and sole Intercessor of the faithful.

Troparia

With the souls of the righteous departed, O Savior, give rest also to the soul of Thy servant; preserving [him,her] in the blessed life that is with Thee, O Lover of Mankind.

In the place of Thy rest, O Lord, where all Thy saints repose, give rest also to the soul of Thy servant, for Thou only lovest mankind.

Glory to the Father, and to the Son, and to the Holy Spirit.

Thou art the God who descended into Hell and loosed the bonds of the captives held there. Grant rest also to the soul of Thy servant.

Now and ever and unto ages of ages. Amen.

O only pure and immaculate Virgin, who gave birth to God without ever knowing man, intercede that the soul of your servant may be saved.

The Litany of the Departed

Priest: Again and again in peace let us pray to the Lord.

People: Lord have mercy!

Priest: Again let us pray for the repose of the blessed child _____ (name), and that according to His unfailing promise, He will grant to [him, her] His heavenly Kingdom.

People: Lord have mercy, Lord have mercy, Lord have mercy!

Priest: Again let us pray that the Lord God will establish [his, her] soul where the Just repose.

People: Lord have mercy, Lord have mercy, Lord have mercy!

Priest: The mercies of God, the kingdom of heaven and rest with the saints, for [him, her] and for ourselves, let us entreat of Christ, our Immortal King and our God.

People: Grant it, O Lord!

Priest: Let us pray to the Lord.

People: Lord have mercy!

Priest: O Lord Jesus Christ our God, Who has promised to bestow the heavenly Kingdom on them born of water and the Spirit, and who, in blamelessness of life have been translated unto You; and who said: "Suffer the little children to come to Me for of such is the Kingdom of Heaven," we humbly pray, according to Your unfailing promise: Grant the inheritance of Your Kingdom to Your servant, the spotless child _____ (name), who now has departed from us. And grant that we may continue to the end in a chaste and Christian life, that we may take up our abode in the heavenly mansions with all Your saints.

For You are the resurrection, the Life and the Repose of all Your servants and of Your servant now departed, the child _____ (name). O Christ our God, and to You we give glory, together with Your eternal Father and Your all-holy, good, and life-creating Spirit, now and ever and unto ages of ages.

People: Amen!

Parting Prayer

Priest: O Lord Jesus, who preserves infants in the present life, and in the life to come prepares for them a place in the bosom of Abraham, and in accordance with their purity a radiant habitation of angels where the souls of the Just repose; accept, O Master, the soul of Your departed servant, the child _____ (name), in peace, for You said, "Suffer the little children to come to me, for of such is the Kingdom of Heaven." For to You is due all glory, honor and worship, together with the Father and the Holy Spirit, now and ever and unto ages of ages.

People: Amen.

Benediction

Priest: May He who rose from the dead and rules over the living and the dead, Christ our true God, through the prayers of His most pure mother and of all the saints, establish the soul of His servant, the child _____ (name), who has been taken from us in the mansions of the righteous, and number [him, her] among the just; and have mercy on us, for He is good and loves mankind.

People: Amen.

Priest: Grant rest eternal in blessed falling asleep, O Lord, to the soul of Thy departed servant, the child _____ (name), and make [his, her] memory to be eternal!

People: Memory eternal! Memory eternal! Memory eternal!

The Suffering and Death of Children[1]

Metropolitan Anthony of Sourozh

Whether we are dealing with children or with grown-ups, in pain or in anguish, we must never forget the people who surround them. Children have parents; grown-ups have wives and families. And it is not always the person who actually suffers who is the most distressed. At times the person who is physically suffering has enough to do to fill his time, to use up all his spiritual opportunities, while the people who are around him, particularly when they feel helpless, have a very complex and distressing time.

I would like to say something about suffering and about the death of children, but what I have to say also applies to a very great extent to parents, to friends, to people who are outside the actual suffering but are concerned with what is going on. We cannot approach the question of suffering and death unless we have an idea, unless we have some sort of evaluation of suffering, of death—and of life. One of the things which makes us so helpless in the face of suffering—of children in particular, but also of grown-ups—is that we have no point of view concerning it. We face situations without having any idea of what we think of the predicament as such. Today it seems to be commonplace to consider suffering as an evil and to think that suffering must be avoided or alleviated or pushed back as completely and as far as possible. The result of this is, I think, the growth of cowardice: people are afraid, and this fear of suffering at times is more disastrous than the suffering itself.

I have spent some fifteen years of my life being a physician, so I have some personal experience of how things work in hospitals and outside them. What usually happens is that people are told: "There is no reason why you should suffer—life should be smooth, things should be good, suffering is an evil." And then when suffering comes our way, most of the people who surround us take it as an injustice on the part of fate, as an event that should not take place. It is probably put together with the various things which are called "acts of

1 Printed in *Sourozh* No. 9, 1984, reprinted by permission of the author.

God" in insurance policies. This is, I think, a remarkable expression, because an "act of God," if you try to define it from the list of things which are called by that name, are things so monstrous, so shocking, that no man would do them—it takes God to do them. In many cases, suffering is regarded in that way. No human would inflict it, and yet God allows it. It is completely evil and wrong, and yet God does not do anything about it. In this way people are deprived both of a manly approach to suffering as such, and of the real help they could derive from God if they did not define him in the first place as the very person who is responsible for all evils.

Sometimes people come to me and express distress at what their life is like. More often than not they explain why they react so wrongly to cicumstances by saying: "Well, God has allowed this and that; I would be a saint if God had not made my life unbearable." Very often, before suggesting absolution, I tell the person: "Now, before you receive God's forgiveness, are you prepared to forgive him for all his misdeeds? Because, from what you have said, quite obviously he is the cause of all evils." Well, this is very much the way in which people react to their own suffering and to the suffering of others around them; and if *that* is the approach, then there is nothing to lean on anyhow.

Now I do not consider suffering and death as good in themselves. But they are not an evil in themselves. Nor are they a one-sided act of divine cruelty: life on earth is something more complex than this. God—his will, his wisdom, and his love—plays a substantial part. The powers of darkness play their part, and man plays his part between the evil that can invade the world and the good that can conquer it. Man has the dread power of allowing either the one or the other to have the upper hand. So that whenever suffering or any other form of evil comes our way, it is not enough to turn to God either accusingly or miserably. We must realise that the situation is defined by human evil as much as by anything else. There is a collective responsibility for particular suffering which we must accept and face together.

When grown-ups suffer, one can, more easily than with children, see the good it can do to them. It is against odds that character is built. It is in the face of suffering that we learn patience, endurance, courage. It is by facing other people's suffering that we can reach a depth of faith, a depth of surrender to which otherwise we could not attain. *Not* to rebel, *not* to protest, but to grow into harmony with the ways of God is something which we cannot achieve without challenge. You re-member the Crucifixion: the way in which the Mother of God stood by the Cross and said not a word in defence of her divine son who was dying. She did not accuse those who had condemned him. She did not turn aggressively against the people who, with curiosity or indif-ference, were surrounding the Cross. She said nothing. She accepted the death of her son with the same perfection of faith and surrender which she had when she accepted the Incarnation. This applies to all of us. The Mother of God in this respect should be for us an image and an example. Throughout the Gospel she is the one who allows her son to go his way. To enter into all the tragedy which is the destiny of the Son of God become Son of Man. This is important for us when someone who is dear to us walks into pain, suffering, anguish.

Now there is in the suffering of children something which is more puzzling, in a way, than in the suffering of grown-ups, because in the suffering of the grown-up we can see the good it might do if the person lived up to the greatness of his vocation. But what about the child? Can a child who suffers learn something which is of real and great value—patience and humility, courage and endurance, faith and surrender? I remember a child whose answer is recorded in the life of one of the French saints of the 18th century. The man asked a child of nine years of age how he managed to endure a very painful illness that eventually killed him, and the child said: "Father (he was nine), I have learnt not to perceive today either yesterday's suffering, nor to anticipate tomorrow's." This is something of which very few grown-ups are capable, because whether it is moral suffering, psychological distress, or physical suffering, what usually makes it so unbearable is that every moment we seem to live and re-live all those past moments of pain and anguish, and at every mo-ment we expect that it will last for ever, will never come to an end, and we cannot face this sum total of all our past suffering and of our future suffering, while more often than not we could face the actual present suffering of our body or of our soul.

This example concerns a child of nine. What about even smaller children, who cannot reason things out in this particular way? Can suffering do something for their eternal soul, or is it sheer nonsense and cruelty? We have a tendency to think that it is through our minds, through our conscious response, through our intellectual elaboration, that we grow in spirit. We imagine that our spiritual life is made of the lofty thoughts and deep feelings which we have developed. This is not our spiritual life. It is that intermediary part of us which is neither the body nor the spirit. I would like to draw an analogy to make myself clearer. We do baptize children. What do we expect, if we expect anything at all? What is the reason why we find it makes sense? Because, consciously or not, we believe that the living spirit, the living soul of this infant, is capable of meeting the living God face to face, apart from any psychological understanding, apart from intellectual or emotional response, a living soul meeting the living God. That the sacraments of the Church address themselves to this living soul which does not depend for its knowledge of God on intelligence, consciousness, and so on.

But if this is true, then it applies also to all those things that happen in the body or soul of a child before it can be intellectually aware of things. As far as grown-ups are concerned, I think, from what I have seen, that it applies to people who are mentally ill, who are beyond reach, who seem to be completely separated from the surrounding world, and whom we meet no longer where we left them but as men and women who have matured and become greater than they were. It is as if behind this screen of folly, of madness, the life of the Spirit has continued, because God cannot be stopped or kept out by what is going on in our intellect or in our emotions. God has direct access. God meets a human being at the level of his soul, that is, ultimately at the level of silence and of those things which are beyond words, at the level of mystery, of those things which can be known within silence but which cannot be expressed by words otherwise than symbolically, which can only be hinted at.

So if a child is ill at a time when we cannot expect that he will consciously be aware of what is going on, or that he will be able to learn those things which require will, intellect, maturity of emotion, an active faith, and active surrender, it does not mean that what is happening to him will not do something, will not be a positive event or a positive contribution to his eternal life. And that, I think, is particularly important for parents and grown-ups to realise when children are beyond reach, like certain intellectually deficient children. There is a limit to communication in words, but there is no limit to communication in other ways. Ultimately, a meeting between a soul and God takes place at the heart of silence. Any meeting between two persons takes place beyond words. It takes place where God is.

In the Orthodox Church we insist that when a woman is pregnant she should make her confession, put her life right, receive Communion, pray, because the relatedness that exists between her and the child is such that what happens to her happens to the child. When the child is born, we expect the parents to pray over it. We give Baptism, Confirmation and Holy Communion to new-born babies for the reasons which I have given before: because the living God can meet his living creature at a depth which is far beyond any ordinary means of communication. When a child is ill, intellectually beyond reach, it still remains that this child can be prayed over, prayed about, held before God. It can also have participation in the sacraments of the Church. If parents and those surrounding such a child realised this more often, if instead of trying to break through a wall that cannot be broken through, they went to that depth where in God we all meet, then there would be a relatedness of which they would be aware, which would be the beginning an eternal relationship. And this applies also to death.

God is not the God of the dead; he is the God of the living. If we live in God we live close to each other, and when a child has departed this life so often the parents have a double sense of distress. On the one hand, the child has died. This would apply also to a grown-up. There is no physical presence, there is no direct, physical relatedness. But also, in a strange way, we imagine that the child that dies, the baby that dies, remains, as it were, a baby for ever, remains out of reach, because on earth it did not evolve that intellect which allows communication and those emotions which bind us together. And yet, if this is a living soul, alive in and by the power of the living God, then if we could only reach out to the depth which is our own soul, our own spirit, we could without fear be certain that nothing can separate us. When the time comes when all things are fulfilled, we will not meet on the level of our psychological richness or poverty, we will meet spirit to spirit and soul to soul. And on this earth we need to be aware of it.

Our relationship with those who have departed this life does not lie in the past; it is not in the future; it is in the present—that split second which the present is, and which is the meeting-point with eternity, that is with God. It is now that we are related to those who have departed this life, and it is true that there is no physical sight, no physical touch; but this is not the level on which we communicate. Even as we are now, when there is between us a real relationship, it is not simply conditioned by our mutual unterstanding of words, of language, of symbols. We have understanding and relationship to the extent to which, soul in soul, we meet in silence, in depth. In a way, real communication begins where the ordinary means of communication have been left aside. Real understanding is beyond words. When children suffer, we must make an act of faith concerning their ability, because they are living souls, to grow into an evern deeper intimacy with God, and we must be certain that what is happening to them is not lost for them. When they depart this life, we must also remember that God is the God of the living.

In all this we should not forget the importance of touch. Touch in relationships. Physical contact. In practically every religious rite things are conveyed by contact. the laying-on of hands, a blessing—so many things are done physically. We should be aware of the spiritual qualities of our bodies. Without our bodies we could not commune in the sacrament of the Body and Blood of Christ. We could not commune with him. It is through our bodies and because of what they represent, because of what they are, that we can have this communion with Christ and God. In human relationships touch plays an immense role. How much one can convey of compassion, of love, of tenderness by putting one's hand on another hand or on a shoulder, which will never be conveyed by words. And with sick children perhaps more than with anyone—or perhaps not, because when a person is ill, gravely, grievously ill, everyone becomes a child again—so much can be conveyed by human touch: sacramental, sacred or simply human (which is also sacred and sacramental). This is something which we must teach the parents of sick children: where words fail, when means of communication are not there, there is a mysterious way of conveying what cannot be conveyed, of expressing with certainty what one is incapable of expressing—love. tenderness, compassion, but also faith and life—by the way in which we treat a body.

We have to deal not only with the child who is ill, but also with those who around him are distressed. And they *must* learn, through faith—instead of being overcome by grief, instead of being conquered and destroyed—that they are sharing in a mystery, in a situation in which each child—and we are all someone's children—in which each child participates, one way or another, in the mystery of the Lord Jesus Christ, who was born into a world of time, out of eternity, in order to die, and through death to open to us unconquerable eternal life.